THE STUDENT
GUIDE TO WRITING:
PLAYWRITING

THE STUDENT GUIDE TO WRITING:
PLAYWRITING

ROB DRUMMER

OLA ANIMASHAWUN

JOHN YORKE

TOM HOLLOWAY

FIN KENNEDY

STEVE WINTER

CAROLINE JESTER

CAROLINE HORTON

LUCY KERBEL

EDITED BY
JENNIFER TUCKETT

CONTENTS

INTRODUCTION

BY JENNIFER TUCKETT

Welcome to *The Student Guide to Writing: Playwriting*. This book is the second in a series between the MA Dramatic Writing at Drama Centre London at Central Saint Martins, one of the top courses in scriptwriting, and Oberon Books, one of the UK's most prestigious performing arts publishers. The partnership aims to provide access to the leading dramatic writing training coming out of the industry for the first time.

Book one was *Dramatic Writing Masterclasses: Key Advice from the Industry Masters*, which began the partnership by providing ten Masterclasses across all forms of dramatic writing. Future books will include in-depth guides to writing film, television, radio and digital media.

For this volume, we have been working in partnership with the Bush Theatre, one of the UK's most successful new writing theatres, and we're delighted to provide access to step-by-step lesson plans for writing a theatre play.

The lessons are written by ten top industry professionals who have led the way in the industry in terms of playwriting training and the book brings together, and publishes, their playwriting teaching for the first time.

These professionals are:

- **ROB DRUMMER**, Artistic Director of Boundless Theatre Company and former Associate Dramaturg at the Bush Theatre

- **OLA ANIMASHAWUN**, founder of the Royal Court Theatre's world famous young writers programme

- **JOHN YORKE**, founder of the BBC Writers Academy, which had one of the biggest impacts as a training programme on dramatic writers' careers in the UK

- **JENNIFER TUCKETT**, Course Leader, MA Dramatic Writing, Drama Centre London at Central Saint Martins and Director of Writers at Work Productions, which manages London Writers' Week amongst other projects

- **TOM HOLLOWAY**, playwright and mentor, nominated by the Bush Theatre

- **FIN KENNEDY**, founder of Schoolwrights and Artistic Director of Tamasha Theatre Company, Britain's foremost touring theatre company

- **STEVE WINTER**, Director of the Kevin Spacey Foundation and co-founder of the Old Vic New Voices 24 Hour Plays and TS Eliot US/UK Exchange, three leading programmes for emerging practitioners

- **CAROLINE JESTER**, Dramaturg and writer, co author of *Playwriting Across the Curriculum* and *Fifty Playwrights on their Craft* and former Dramaturg at Birmingham Repertory Theatre

- **CAROLINE HORTON**, writer, performer, director and mentor, nominated by the Bush Theatre, who has led the way in terms of experimental work

- **LUCY KERBEL**, Director of Tonic Theatre, a company celebrated for its work in terms of gender equality, and founder of the Platform project for writing for young audiences

We hope the lesson plans in this book can be used individually by writers or students to build up a play or can be used by teachers at school or university level or in the industry to teach playwriting and to help students or writers create a script. Each plan contains exercises which are flexible in terms of length or class size, or you can follow the lessons on your own as quickly or as slowly as you'd like.

The final two lesson plans cover some of the key advice on the business side of being a playwright as well.

In addition, the second half of the book contains work by the five student winners of The Student Guide to Writing: Playwriting competition. This competition ran as stage one of this project to provide access to the best training coming out of the industry for the first time and was open to students at schools and universities and writers across the UK. You can perform this work by contacting Oberon Books and/or we hope you can use the winners' work as an example of the lessons, exploring on your own or in a class how it uses the teaching methods.

Finally, why are we doing this series? Well, it seemed to us that, for a long time, a lot of industry training has gone unpublished so if you can't get onto a scheme, you don't know what is being taught. Similarly, it's sometimes difficult to get onto that programme without knowing what is being taught so this can be vicious cycle. We hope this new series of guides will address this and mean that anyone can access this advice.

Thank you for reading *The Student Guide to Writing: Playwriting* and we hope you enjoy building up your theatre play.

PART ONE
THE LESSON PLANS

LESSON PLAN ONE
GETTING STARTED

BY ROB DRUMMER, ARTISTIC DIRECTOR, BOUNDLESS THEATRE

Please Note: This lesson plan can be followed individually or taught to a group, either way I have suggested timings for the exercises to keep you on track and to get the most from writing quickly.

I. FOCUS:

This lesson plan is focused on getting started and the very beginning of writing a play. I will offer some ideas and advice as well as exercises to get you going and to demonstrate how story might work in your play. The objective of this lesson plan is to be able to understand what a play is, what it might look like and to demonstrate ways of starting out when considering a new story and the early stages of playwriting and to offer some general advice before you begin writing your play.

2. WHY THIS AREA OF CRAFT IS IMPORTANT:

Before we begin work on your play, I hope it's useful to share my key advice.

It might be helpful to start with what a play is, in its simplest form, so how about the following definition:

"A play is a form of literature written by a playwright, usually consisting of dialogue between characters, intended for theatrical performance rather than just reading."

The most important thing here is to remember that a play is intended for performance, to be experienced by an audience and to be performed by actors, so the words on the page are only the beginning. They are like the plans for a building or even a sketch prepared before a painting. A lot of the making of a new play happens with the script as a starting point, even when all of the dialogue is spoken. Remember, as a playwright you are telling stories with words and pictures.

I like to also consider what a playwright is, so how about the following definition:

If you think about how the word playwright is spelt it has more in common with a shipwright or a wheelwright and that is to say that they are both makers, contributing to a much larger process. The playwright is vital but also is one of the collaborators in the making of the play.

In my experience we all write differently, I've yet to meet two playwrights who mirror each other's writing habits or who approach writing plays in identical ways. Of course there are shared ways of working and similarities and one thing that is the same across the board is that we all need to start somewhere.

It is fair to say that plays come in all shapes and sizes and the more you read the more you will realize there are lots of ways to write, to arrange your writing on the page but there are some rules you could start to follow.

3. A SIMPLE EXERCISE OR EXERCISES TO DEVELOP YOUR PLAY:

I. SOME WAYS TO FORMAT YOUR PLAY ON THE PAGE

I'm going to begin with some advice in terms of formatting:

1. Start each new line of dialogue on a new line and include the character name at the start of the line.
2. If you are using stage directions, separate them from dialogue on the page and perhaps use italics, less is usually more and keep them limited to essential action that is vital to the storytelling.
3. Generally speaking, a big shift in time or location means a new scene might be useful, have a think about time and place and make a decision if your play works best with a break in the middle (the interval) or if it is best experienced in one sitting, over ninety minutes.
4. Consider the sound of your dialogue, the rhythm and pace of your play and think about characters who might interrupt each other, or might trail off at the end of a sentence. Some interesting ways to represent this include:

    … represents a character trailing off at the end of a sentence, perhaps lost in thought.

    / represents a point of interruption, where the next character overlaps with their dialogue

5. Finally, always remember that page numbers are really helpful, your name and the title of the play should appear at least on the cover page and a character breakdown can be really helpful to anybody reading your play for the first time.

2. THINKING ABOUT WHAT YOU WANT TO WRITE ABOUT

So, now you have an idea of what a play is and that a playwright is one of many collaborators, as well as some tips for arranging your play on the page, what do you write about? What follows are three ways to get a conversation started around telling stories and three exercises I return to time and time again when writing or developing new plays.

1.   WHAT'S GOING ON?

Theatre has the ability to respond relatively quickly to what is going on in the world, (far quicker than TV or film for example) and as a result plays often have a social or political starting point or issue at their heart. Although I think the best plays tackle single issues with complexity and subtlety it isn't a bad idea to train yourself to have opinions on what is going on in the world. I often use the following exercise to check in on the issues that I am more concerned with and think it is a great way to get started:

Give yourself ten minutes to come up with three answers for each of the below and a further ten minutes to discuss (or to brainstorm why these are your answers if you are working on your own). You can always break a larger group into three separate groups and give them one of the issues each and have a larger discussion. You might want to develop the exercise further and shortlist the most important issues, one from each group and then have a go at pitching a story that incorporates all three answers.

Three biggest global issues

Three biggest national issues

Three biggest personal issues

2.   THE LAST SEVEN DAYS

Think back over the last seven days of your life, trying to remember the major events, turning points, discoveries and new experiences. Take your time to think about what was significant about the last seven days (even if you feel as if nothing has happened, force yourself to make some decisions).

What is important here is to break the past seven days into a series of events that caused something to change, think of them as events that caused you to take action, or to move in a different direction, in an active way, an example could be:

> *Monday: My mum had to stay late at work, I needed to collect my younger brother from school, where I met an old friend I hadn't seen for a long time. We arrange to meet later in the week, which has opened a can of worms for me, forcing me to confront the past when…*

Okay, so the example starts getting a little fanciful and yet it should demonstrate how one seemingly small event can bring about dramatic possibility. If we were to continue the sentence, what happened in the past becomes an important consideration and could drive the beginning of a story.

Have a go at thinking about all of the events, at least one a day that brought about a small or big change in your life over the past seven days.

> Note: Give ten minutes, to think and note the events and a further five to discuss in pairs. Then allow enough time to discuss as a larger group or if working on your own, ensure you have at least seven events and in a final five minutes, make a note of the consequence of each event (what happened as a result of the event, the action).

3. <u>WHAT HAPPENS AT THE END?</u>

With all this talk of getting started, I often find it important to think about the end. Pixar, who are some of the best storytellers working today, encourage writers to think about where the story ends, as endings are difficult. Often, leaving the ending to be discovered can result in a play that loses its direction and, in my experience, the middle of the story is a lot easier to tackle if there's a sense of where it might end.

4. A SIMPLE CHARACTER EXERCISE:

Finally, I'd like to move on to a simple character exercise. Stories happen because the characters want something, there's an obstacle and they need to do something to overcome it to achieve the thing they want. Therefore in my opinion it is the characters in a play that give us everything and when we are starting out I suggest a great place to begin is thinking about who you are writing about.

Here is a very simple character exercise to get a story started:

STEP ONE (five minutes)

Think about two characters (A and B) and answer the following questions about them below:

Character A   what do they want, what's in their way, what's their secret?

Character B   how are they the obstacle to A's want? What lie have they told and what happens if it comes out?

STEP TWO (five minutes)

Now take both of the characters and put them in a room together (you might want to think about details such as time of day, the type of room, what is going on outside).

STEP THREE (five minutes)

Continue the dialogue that I have started for you below:

A: Why am I only hearing about this now?

B:

Note: If working in a larger group, take fifteen minutes to read the dialogue, at least three examples, and start a discussion about what the characters want, their obstacles and secret etc. The objective is to reveal as much of the information as possible in the dialogue in interesting ways.

■ ■ ■

What the above exercise should help you explore as you are getting started is how to create dramatic action out of conflict in your play. It is important that your play contains events that add up to action, as it is the dramatic action and conflict in your play that will keep the audience engaged. The simplest way to create more conflict is to ensure that your characters want something but something is in their way, especially if this thing is another character, then the effort to achieve their want is the dramatic action of your play.

The next most important thing to consider at the beginning is the central question in your play. Be prepared for this to develop as you write and perhaps it will change all together but to think about a question at the beginning of your writing will keep you focused as you start to tell the story.

> Tip: Keep the central question of your play in sight, on a piece of paper above your computer as you write so that you are always considering your audience and ensuring that they are being posed a question through your play.

One great way to get the creativity flowing is answering the following questions with a single sentence:

1. What happens in your story?
2. Where does your story happen?
3. When does your story happen?
4. Why does your story happen? What causes events?

Finally, once you have written that first draft of your play read it aloud then put it aside for a day or so. When you return to it, read it again and when you've finished write a one paragraph story synopsis of 100 words. Then looking back over the 100 words have a go at reducing the synopsis to a sentence. Once you have this, read it and then cut the sentence down to seven words, then three words. Finally, no surprises here, take the three words and reduce to a single word. The trick here is to not simply edit words out but to try and keep representing the whole story of your play, you can use new words and you don't have to worry about making sense beyond the sentence stage of the exercise.

5.   FINAL ADVICE:

Have people read your work aloud. They don't have to be actors, hearing it will help you massively. Playwriting is about telling story through dialogue so hearing it read will be an important test of the story.

Always think about your audience, sit down with somebody who hasn't read your play, and describe the story to them. Do they get bored, when are they excited, what are they curious about?

Think about your perspective on the world – often people say write what you know. Sometimes this can be misunderstood as tell your own story, which isn't always interesting. Instead see this as about writing from your perspective, through your eyes, your ears, what can you write about the world we live in today?

Have two types of people read your work, someone close and someone not close. One will help you keep writing. The other will make you a better writer.

Get into the habit of writing. If you're short on time, try writing little but often.

Overwrite, then cut.

Bad writing is okay. Get the story out. Get it written. Then make it better over as many drafts as you need. Keep hearing it. Be prepared to kill the best ideas in pursuit of the best story.

Ask yourself what your story is. You could try summarizing it in a sentence or two and sticking it by your desk, so you can keep it in mind. Keep returning to it. Keep it fresh in your mind.

LESSON PLAN TWO
IDEAS

BY OLA ANIMASHAWUN, FOUNDER OF THE ROYAL COURT THEATRE'S
YOUNG WRITERS PROGRAMME

Now you have explored getting started and got some top tips on this, we are now going to move on to your play and think about Ideas, helping you find an idea for your play.

1. FOCUS:

This lesson plan is about Ideas – focusing on writing about something you feel passionate about, as the source and inspiration for the bedrock of your play.

2. WHY THIS AREA OF CRAFT IS IMPORTANT:

Your passion is important because if you choose to write about something you really care about, it will be likely that it's something you've already thought about a great deal and therefore the chances are it will be a subject you already know a lot about. Plus, writing from your heart greatly increases the chances of you finishing, because you'll be using your play to say something you think is really important to be said.

3. A SIMPLE EXERCISE OR EXERCISES TO DEVELOP YOUR PLAY:

The following exercise is based around the principle of automatic writing.

Some pointers before you start:

You should find a quiet space and a moment in your day where you know you are not going to be interrupted or disturbed.

Take a minute to try and empty your mind of the clutter and tensions of everyday life – relax, try and breathe deeply and evenly and only start when you're ready.

When you write you are writing for your eyes only – you will never be under any compulsion to share anything you've written in this exercise – you are doing this writing purely for yourself.

Thus, don't censor yourself at all, be brave, challenge yourself to be as honest and open with yourself as you can – if you think it, write it down – and make this note to yourself – if there are any areas you know you are straying away from or being cautious about – you don't have to go into them, but simply make conscious recognition that this is what you are doing.

Try and write for the full amount of time without stopping or taking your pen off the page – if you get stuck, simply write I am writing about… (the given subject) over and over again…until the next new thought comes to you or you run out of time.

So now spend a minute of free writing on each of the following prompts:

1. What makes you angry?
2. What frightens you?
3. What gives you hope?
4. What do you think that you'd never say out loud?
5. What makes you sad?
6. What makes you happy?

Remember, this writing is private. Save this writing for your own and future reference. Make a note of anything that surprised you or interested you in any way for whatever reason.

Now – from these responses – choose one of them to continue writing about for a further five minutes. Remember, at this stage you can write in any way, or any style, just don't censor yourself – see where it takes you and what it unlocks for you.

Another quick writing exercise that compliments the exercise above:

If good plays consist of conflict and struggle, which they do, then take five minutes to make a list of things you have struggled with in life and where you have experienced conflict.

As a result of carrying out these exercises, you will hopefully have begun to discover the things you really care about and where your passion lies, and in the process, thus begun to have identified the likely subject for your play.

Now, imagine that this play might be the last thing you ever get the chance to write. What are you going to write about? What is it that is so important, that you must communicate through your play, as your final statement to the world through your writing?

Now, make a note of what the idea for your play is.

Optional step: if you are using this lesson plan in a longer class or you have more time, you may like to take this one step further before you go onto structure, by sharing your idea with a partner and explaining why you feel so passionate about it.

Now, in terms of your subject and theme, think of a character who is lacking in something and therefore wants something deeply in relation to your theme.

E.g. you might feel passionately about capital punishment and question its morality. Thus you might create a character who is in jail and is facing the prospect of imminent execution for their crime.

Now think of another character who is somehow related to your first character, i.e. they know each other and are NOT strangers meeting for the first time.

Note the two characters are in conflict with each other for some reason.

Both characters want something from each other – decide what it is, remembering to keep your theme and overall idea in mind.

Thus, in my example, the second character might be a lawyer, desperate for her client to reveal a vital piece of evidence to them, but for some reason the client doesn't want to tell them.

Now write a simple scene showing what happens in this encounter. The scene will end when one of the characters leaves the location. By the end of the scene at least one of the characters will have changed in some way.

Share your scene with a partner and the class and ask them what they liked about the scene, and if they had any further questions about it.

4. FINAL ADVICE:

I once noted the following advice from a writer, who commented that probably the most productive place to look for ideas is in your own personal life experience, because:

1. Your world is one you know very well – better than anyone else – and you are the only person with unique and exclusive access to your experience

2. What you draw from that world will undoubtedly be the things you have the strongest feelings about

3. Although the specific detail of your experience will be unique and singular, the themes and the chords your story will inevitably strike will have a universal resonance. The audience will recognize and connect with the action and the events where they prompt the recollection and recognition of incidents, characters, behaviour and occurrences in their own lives.

LESSON PLAN THREE
STRUCTURE

BY JOHN YORKE, FOUNDER OF THE BBC WRITERS ACADEMY
AND AUTHOR OF *INTO THE WOODS*

I. FOCUS:

This lesson plan is focused on Structure. All stories have a shape, and more often than not that same shape can be found in every archetypal story – not just in theatre or television drama, but in every form of narrative. The idea of this lesson is to introduce you to the basic ingredients of that structure.

2. WHY THIS AREA OF CRAFT IS IMPORTANT:

There are no successful writers who haven't mastered structure. However, it's important to understand that that doesn't mean all those writers have studied it. What this suggests is that structure isn't some external construct imposed from studying, for example, Robert McKee, but rather something that comes from within. Structure is something the human brain imposes on random events to give them shape (that's what stories are – order from chaos), with that shape giving those events meaning. So you don't HAVE to study it, but studying it won't do you any harm – the more you learn about your craft the easier and more fascinating it will be.

3. A SIMPLE EXERCISE OR EXERCISES TO DEVELOP YOUR PLAY:

Take a simple fairy tale such as *Jack and the Beanstalk*. Structure normally consists of three acts – beginning, middle and end. Divide *Jack and the Beanstalk* into three acts.

The first act is the beginning of the adventure – the invitation into a strange new world. In James Bond it's when M gives him his mission, in *Alice in Wonderland* it's where she falls down rabbit hole. Where is it in *Jack and the Beanstalk*? When is Jack invited to join a strange new world?

The second act is the journey through that strange new world. It's strange, and exciting and normally ends with a crisis – the hero finding themselves captured or in great danger. James Bond is captured – Alice faces the evil queen of hearts. During this act the hero/heroine often learns or gets hold of something they never knew before. What does Jack get hold of? Does he learn anything? When does he face his maximum crisis? His peak jeopardy?

The third act is the final battle in which the hero or protagonist overcomes their enemy or antagonist. They are rewarded if it's a happy ending, or punished if it's a tragedy. How is James Bond rewarded? How is Jack rewarded?

Once you've worked out the structure of the fairytale, try and transpose it into the modern day. You'll be surprised how many modern stories are similar. The latest Star Wars film *The Force Awakens* is a good example. Rey's beanstalk is the Millennium Falcon. What she finds in the middle, the object she has to master, is Luke Skywalker's light sabre and what it represents. That's one example. What if Jack is a poor kid with no friends? What could be the equivalent of a beanstalk, what could be the equivalent of the golden egg? Use your imagination – there are no right answers.

Now make a note for your play which you came up with the idea for via the last lesson plan (or you can come up with your idea now) of what your three act structure would look like for this play:

1.   Act One – the beginning of the adventure

2.   Act Two – the journey through the strange new world

3.   Act Three – the final battle

Optional exercise for more advanced writers:

Once you understand three-act structure, ask yourself "Why did Shakespeare write five acts?" There are a number of reasons – the plays were relatively long, the seating (or standing) was primitive and uncomfortable so it made sense to have more breaks, and once the plays moved indoors each act was the length of the time it took the candles used to light them to burn. In Shakespeare's day five-act drama was very much the norm.

Fundamentally three-act and five act structure are very similar. The first and last acts of both are identical, while the middle act is simply divided into three by giving it two more breaks. What this allows you to do is see more readily just how story structure works.

So how does it work?

There are five key stages in every story, each corresponding to an act:

1. Call to action
2. Things go well, initial objective achieved
3. Things start to go wrong
4. Things go really badly wrong, precipitating crisis
5. Final battle with matters resolved for good or ill

So in a James Bond Film you'd see the following stages:

1. Baddie does great evil. M gives Bond his mission – kill the baddie
2. Bond investigates and gets breakthrough – often finding where villain is
3. Bond finds out true nature of villain, often in villain's lair
4. Bond punished. All hope lost
5. Bond escapes, kills his antagonist and is rewarded with beautiful woman

How does this work in *Goldfinger*? Bearing in mind it's a tragedy, how does this work in *Macbeth* or *The Godfather*?

Have a look at *Jack and the Beanstalk* again – the original fairy tale. How do the five stages or acts fit, bearing in mind that the first and last acts will be the same?

What you should start to notice is that something really important happens in the middle of the story. In the middle of *Goldfinger* Bond is captured, strapped to a bed while a laser beam makes its way up between his legs. He learns just how evil Goldfinger is. In *Macbeth*, he kills his friend Banquo but Banquo's son escapes. In both the heroes learn key knowledge – Bond learns that Goldfinger is a psychopathic sadist bent on world domination, Macbeth that he will have to kill again and again. For both of them there is no going back. In *The Force Awakens*, Rey gets the light sabre half way through. At exactly the same point in *Titanic* the ship hits the iceberg. What happens exactly halfway through *The Godfather*?

How about *Jack and the Beanstalk*? What is the key turning point – the thing that Jack gets or steals halfway through the story?

Screenwriters call this the Midpoint. It's the moment where the hero discovers, or starts to discover, key knowledge about themselves or the world they're now in. What five-act structure reveals then, is that stories tend to be symmetrical. Heroes start with a flaw, half way through they learn or take something, and in the second half they learn how to utilize or keep the thing they've taken or learned. If you go back to our original five-act description:

1. Call to action
2. Things go well, initial objective achieved
3. Things start to go wrong
4. Things go really badly wrong, precipitating crisis
5. Final battle with matters resolved for good or ill

What you'll find is that things don't go wrong immediately in the third act, rather their fortunes peak in the middle – and at midpoint the heroes actions cause the forces of antagonism to massively increase.

How does this happen in *Goldfinger*?, *Titanic*?, *Macbeth*?

So fortunes peak exactly half way through a script. It is this shape that gives rise to the phrase "dramatic arc".

Bearing this in mind EITHER re-write your version of *Jack and the Beanstalk* in five acts – or take another fairy tale like *Hansel and Gretel* and do the same.

Once you have done this, plan your own play you have been working on using the five act structure and make a note of what each of these moments are:

1. Call to action
2. Things go well, initial objective achieved
3. Things start to go wrong
4. Things go really badly wrong, precipitating crisis
5. Final battle with matters resolved for good or ill

4. FINAL ADVICE

Don't get hung up about structure. In the end it's about framing a story so it's both exciting and easy to follow. Think of the most enjoyable mainstream films you've seen. How does their structure compare with *Jack and the Beanstalk*? Try and work out the structure of all your favourite films and plays.

LESSON PLAN FOUR
SCENES

BY JENNIFER TUCKETT, COURSE LEADER, MA DRAMATIC WRITING
AT DRAMA CENTRE LONDON AT CENTRAL SAINT MARTINS

I. FOCUS:

This lesson plan is focused on Scenes, which are the building blocks of plays – scenes are what hold your overall structure together and break it into manageable chunks.

2. WHY THIS AREA OF CRAFT IS IMPORTANT:

Scenes are important because they are what divide your overall structure into sections and allow us to control our plays and how our plays work.

Most plays are divided into scenes, which are marked with scene headings for example:

Scene One

Scene Two

Etc.

Sometimes scenes are unmarked in a play (so the play seems continuous but really the action is made up of hidden scenes, there are just no scene headings).

In either situation, scenes are important as:

1. They create your overall structure and put it into practice
2. They hold our attention by providing changes from one scene to another to progress the action and take us in new and unexpected directions
3. As writers, they are also important as they allow you to control your play by breaking it into manageable chunks

3. A SIMPLE EXERCISE OR EXERCISES TO DEVELOP YOUR PLAY:

1. If you are using this lesson plan in a class or working on your own, begin by brainstorming what scenes are and why you think they are important.

2. Once you have done this, look at a couple of examples to see scenes in action – I recommend the first scene of Laura Wade's play *Colder Than Here* and the first scene of Adam Brace's play *Stovepipe* as good examples of opening scenes – what do you notice about them?

3. We are now going to do the best exercise I know in terms of scenes which is:

Want

Conflict

Event

4. This is what I have found to be a great scene structure which you see in a lot of successful scenes, for example

Colder Than Here, Scene One:

Want: Myra wants to know if this is a good burial ground

Conflict: Jenna doesn't want to be there

Event (this is a change which happens at the end of a scene to send things in a new direction to make us want to read or watch on): At the end of scene one, they decide this isn't the right burial ground and to find another.

I believe these are the key ingredients for a good scene as:

The 'want' makes us want to read or watch on to see if the character is going to get their 'want' or not

The 'conflict' puts the want in jeopardy. If we think the character might not get their want we're compelled to read or watch further.

The 'event' changes things at the end of the scene to make us want to read or watch on to the next scene and further the plot.

5. Here is a simple exercise to help you develop your play using want, conflict and event.

• First, make a note of how long you want your play to be.

• Now make a note of how many scenes you want to be in your play. A scene can be anything from one minute to as long as you want, although I find with scenes of over five minutes it becomes difficult to hold our attention, and often longer scenes are actually divided into several scenes without scene headings (see section two for an explanation of hidden scenes). For the novice playwright, I think around two – five minutes is a good length for a scene. For a short play, it is also fine if there is only one scene per act.

- Finally, now you have made a note of how long your play is and how many scenes you want, make a note of your act headings from the last lesson plan:

  i.e.; Act One: Call to Action etc.

6. You can now start filling in your scenes and planning the want, conflict and event for each scene i.e.:

Act One: Call to action:

Scene One

Want:

Conflict:

Event:

Scene Two

Want:

Conflict:

Event:

Act Two: Things go well

Scene One

Want:

Conflict:

Event:

Scene Two

Want:

Conflict:

Event:

Etc.

At the end of the process, you should have something that looks like this:

Act One: call to action: Lucy wants to save the world (or whatever it is your main character wants)

Scene One:

Want: Lucy, aged fifteen, wants to watch TV

Conflict: Her mum wants to show her the newspaper

Event: Lucy sees the paper says the world is going to end and decides to save the world

Act Two: things go well: Lucy begins to research how to save the world

Scene One:

Want: Lucy wants to research how to save the world

Conflict: The librarian thinks she is messing around

Event: Lucy discovers the best way to make a change is to contact your government so she decides to go to 10 Downing Street

Etc.

7. When you have finished, share your notes with a partner (if you are working in class) or with a friend (if you are working on your own). The person listening should say two things they like and two questions or suggestions for improvement they have.

8. Now revise your notes.

9. Finally, if you want, you can now type this up into a one page outline (prose) now you know your whole story – this will help you clarify exactly what your story is.

10. You are now at the end of the planning process and ready to start fleshing out your play in terms of characterization and dialogue and getting ready to write!

4. FINAL ADVICE

Scenes are often the hardest part of the planning process – it can seem hard, laborious and/or overly technical to work out the length of your play and how many scenes you have and what the want, conflict, and event is for each scene. If you do this work now however, it will make your play much easier to write and ensure that at all times our attention is held and that you are telling your story in the best possible way.

I once heard one of my mentors say that playwriting is made up of left brain (the planning side) and right brain (the writing side). I agree! Once you start writing, you might change your plan slightly but you will have a strong starting point and ensure you are heading in the right direction, saving you time later on.

4

LESSON PLAN FIVE
CHARACTERISATION

BY TOM HOLLOWAY, PLAYWRIGHT AND MENTOR
NOMINATED BY THE BUSH THEATRE

I. FOCUS:

This lesson will be focused on the development of character. We will look at what character means, why it is important and how it is an essential part of any piece of theatre, even when on first glance it might seem absent.

The exercises in this lesson will help you build an entire life for a character before the point of time the play takes place and during it.

Another thing we will look at, and an element of writing I firmly believe in for all stages of creating a play, is the importance of not editing in your head, but getting the work on the page. It is only once it is on the page that we can really judge it and develop our work further. The exercises I suggest are about writing quickly and writing a lot, and then reflecting on what has been written later.

2. WHY THIS AREA OF CRAFT IS IMPORTANT:

CHARACTER'S RELATIONSHIP TO PLAYS

Before we can talk of the importance of character we need to look at some essential elements of a play. There are two things every play must be about:

1. People
2. Conflict

Whether it is Beckett, Kane, Albee, or Miller, every play that has ever been written has these two elements at their core. The works that seem almost devoid of narrative (although I dispute that any work is truly devoid of narrative), still have people and conflict sitting at their heart. If you are writing a play with two penguins on stage, you are still writing about people and conflict.

This means that character is one of the two essential elements of playwriting, and so a piece of theatre cannot exist without it.

Whether you give your characters full names, simply letters for names, or no names at all, you still need to develop them as fully conceived humans (even if in the form of penguins) with flaws and strengths and desires and fears.

CHARACTER'S RELATIONSHIP TO STORY

The next thing we must look at before developing our characters, is the most basic story structure that exists. Not only is this the most basic story structure, it is also in fact the structure of every story that has ever been told:

1. A Character exists in an environment
2. They want/need something
3. Something or someone gets in the way of what they want
4. They either succeed or fail in getting what they want, but they learn something along the way.

From *Gilgamesh* to the works of Charlie Kauffman, this structure holds true. Most questions are asked about '4'. Some say 'but what if the point is that my character hasn't learnt from their mistakes?' The major thing to remember is that your character *must* be different at the end of your play than the beginning. They *must* have gone on a journey. Even if this journey is a rejection of change, conscious or otherwise, they *need* to have been faced with something life changing during your play. Perhaps at the start they think they can change, only to realize they can't or don't want to. This is still a journey and still makes them different at the end to the beginning.

I would also say that the structure above should exist for every one of your characters, from your main character down to your smallest. The scale of what they want/need might be different, but to make them feel well rounded they still need a journey like this. A waiter might simply need to take another character's order, but the character is too busy talking to someone else. The waiter then either succeeds or fails in getting the order, but they've learnt something about their skills, or the annoying nature of the customer, along the way.

CHARACTER'S RELATIONSHIP TO CONFLICT

And finally we must think about what conflict means to our character. I think a mistake we can often make as playwrights is that we give a lot of attention to the large conflict a character faces, but forget that there are layers of conflict, just as there are in every day life. In fact to go a step further, it is actually how our characters respond to small, everyday conflicts (having to wait for an occupied toilet… Trying to get a waiter's attention…

Running for a bus they're not going to catch…) via which we can get a deeper understanding of the character's main needs. How our character responds to just missing a bus will also tell us how they are coping with the cancer diagnosis they have just received, for instance. Continually placing our characters in situations of smaller everyday conflicts lets us do the important job of showing and not telling. It also lets us map the journey of our stories more, and also stretch time out before our characters come head to head with their main needs and the struggle to fulfill them.

3. A SIMPLE EXERCISE OR EXERCISES TO DEVELOP YOUR PLAY:

Before we start looking at these exercises, I'd like to request something of you. When you do these exercises, do them quickly. Give yourself perhaps a minute to answer each once. Set a stopwatch even. And simply follow the first impulse you have. Don't think. Just write.

EXERCISE ONE: BUILDING A LIFE FOR OUR CHARACTER

For this exercise, choose one of the characters from your play you are writing. Remember, just write down the first thing that comes to mind. Don't edit in your head. Follow your impulse. Editing can come later. Only go up to the age that your character is at the end of their play for this exercise – this is important so you don't spoil the sense of anticipation the end of plays often create about where the character is going to go next.

1. Write down one surprising feature of your character's birth. Were they born early? Was the labour long and hard? Were they born by Caesarean section? Was the birth in a hospital or somewhere else? Was the baby in danger? Was the mother in danger? Did the mother survive? Was the father there? Etc.…

2. Write down one surprising thing that happens to your character from birth to age ten. Is it starting school and if so, what about it? Is it moving home, and if so what about it? Does a parent die, and if so what about it? Do the parents divorce and if so, what about it? Do the character make a friend and if so what about it? Etc.…

3. Write down one surprising thing that happens to your character from the ages of ten to twenty. Is it about them leaving school and if so, what about it? Is it about them losing their virginity and if so, what about it? Is it about their first job and if so, what about it? Is it about their first experience of alcohol/drugs and if so, what about it? Etc.…

4. Write down one surprising thing that happens to your character between the ages of twenty and thirty. Is it finishing university and if so, what about it? Is it about falling in love and if so, what about it? Is it about a first betrayal and if so, what about it? Etc.…

5. Write down one surprising thing that happens to your character between the ages of thirty and forty. Do they get divorced and if so, what about it? Do they have a child and if so, what about it? Do they lose their job and if so, what about it? Etc.…

6. Write down one surprising thing that happens to your character between the ages of forty and fifty. Do they get sick and if so, what about it? Do they have an affair and if so, what about it? Do they travel and if so, what about it? Etc.…

7. Write down one thing that happens to your character between the ages of fifty and seventy (note the difference here, and I'm also not trying to say that not many interesting things happen to old people!). Do they retire and if so, what about it? Do they fall in love and if so, what about it? Do they get sick and if so, what about it? Etc.…

8. Now, if you haven't already, write one surprising thing about your character's death. Perhaps they died at an earlier age, or perhaps they have lived into their seventies. Either way, did they die of sickness and if so, what about it? Did they die of an accident and if so, what about it? Did they take their own life or were they murdered and if so, what about it? Etc.

You now know something about the birth of your character, their entire life and even their death. Some of what you've written might seem to conflict with other parts you've written. This is good. This is what life is really like.

Now that you know all this about your character, write for one minute, and only one minute about your reflections on who you think your character is, what kind of person they are, their struggles and strengths, things like that. Again, don't think, just write.

EXERCISE TWO: THE BEST AND WORST THINGS THAT CAN HAPPEN TO YOUR CHARACTER

We need to learn what our character wants and what they fear. This is about mapping the journey of conflict and effort for our characters. One danger in playwriting is that we jump too quickly to the major drama a character faces without necessarily earning that. This exercise should help prevent this.

Again write quickly. Write the first thing that comes to you. Do not edit in your head. In fact until you have a first draft of a script, you should NEVER edit in your head.

1. What is the best thing that could ever happen to your character? Perhaps they win the lottery, for instance.

2. What is something that could make the best thing happen? They win the lottery because they bought a ticket.

3. What is something that could make the thing happen that makes the best thing happen? They buy a lottery ticket because they were in a news agent and needed a pick-me-up.

4. What is something that could make the thing happen that makes the thing happen that makes the best thing happen? They needed a pick-me-up because they just found out their partner was leaving them for someone much younger and much more beautiful.

5. What is something that could make the thing happen that makes the things happen that makes the thing happen that makes the best thing happen? Their partner left them for someone younger and more beautiful because they had spent years in a problematic relationship with someone they never should have been with in the first place.

Obviously your choices will be far more interesting than my examples.

1. What is the worst thing that could ever happen to your character? Perhaps they are fired from their job, for instance.

2. What is something that could make the worst thing happen? They were fired from their job because they were stealing from the workplace.

3. What is something that could make the thing happen that makes the worst thing happen? They are stealing from their job because they have a gambling problem.

4. What is something that could happen that would make the thing happen that makes the thing happen that makes the worst thing happen? They have a gambling problem because of a mix of being prone to addiction and currently facing a lot of unhappiness in their life.

5. What is something that could happen that would make the thing happen that makes the thing happen that makes the thing happen that makes the worst thing happen? They are currently facing a lot of unhappiness in their life because they have found out their partner is cheating on them.

Through going through these two sets of steps (and ignoring my examples as much as possible!) you now know what is the best and worst thing that could happen to your character. This best and worst thing might not actually be your character's biggest desires and fears, but they will definitely help you work out what those desires and fears are. For instance, in my examples, the first character doesn't necessarily want to win the lottery, but they do want to be out of a loveless relationship and be able to start their life again. And in terms of fears, my character's biggest fear might not be losing their job, but in fact that their partner is cheating on them and they're going to have to try to leave them and start a new life.

5

The other thing this exercise allows us to do is think about layers of conflict. If you think about my examples from the worst thing that could happen, my character might be sitting in the meeting where they're losing their job, while also worried about the gambling debts they've incurred, while also worrying about their partner being unfaithful to them. If I was to try to develop this scene further, because these conflicts are already so big, I would think about smaller conflicts I can bring in to the scene. As well as all this does my character need to go to the toilet, while being told they're fired? Is English their second language so they're struggling to follow what their boss is telling them, all the while facing the worry of the gambling debts and the potentially unfaithful lover? Does the meeting with the boss keep getting interrupted by the boss' secretary trying to get some signatures from the boss? How my character responds to these interruptions will tell me how they feel about being fired and therefore how they feel about the debts and their lover. If they're avoiding coming to terms with the state they're in, they might be fine with the interruptions, for instance.

4. FINAL ADVICE

A teacher once said to me that every character should always be 'on the edge of disaster'. I love this term. Whenever you are developing your character, keep asking yourself this question, and if there are times they seem not to be on the edge of disaster, see what you can do to get them back there. And remember, there are small and large disasters. Don't forget the small ones, and in fact use them to highlight the large one.

Also, although I have found these exercises useful at times, I also often don't use them at all. I find my characters through putting them in scenes and seeing how they respond. One scene leads to another.

LESSON PLAN SIX
DIALOGUE

BY FIN KENNEDY, FOUNDER OF SCHOOLWRIGHTS AND
ARTISTIC DIRECTOR OF TAMASHA THEATRE COMPANY

I. FOCUS:

This lesson plan is focused on Dialogue, which is important because alongside movement, physicality and the decisions they make, it is the primary vehicle by which characters in a play express Action – what they want – which is the key driver in moving forward most dramatic plots.

Contrary to popular belief, writing Drama isn't actually about writing words on a page at all, it is about arranging events in time and space – doing, not saying, is the true language of Drama (this is also where the 'wright' in 'playwright' comes from). That isn't to say Dialogue isn't important – it undoubtedly is – but it is and should always be subservient to Action and the requirements of the plot. In that sense, what is not said is equally as important (sometimes more so) than what is said. Harold Pinter was as famous for his pauses as his sparse, muscular dialogue.

Unlike in novels, where writers have the luxury of giving the reader access to a running commentary on everything their characters are thinking and feeling, in plays the writer has only what a character says and does, with no omniscient voice. The temptation is to over-explain, to have characters tell each other everything because the inexperienced playwright does not trust the audience to keep up. They will – and what's more they will enjoy having information withheld. It means they have to lean in. Counter-intuitively, temporarily excluding your audience is the secret to actively engaging them in your world. (The re-writing process is often about going back over an over-written scene and tucking all the subtext back beneath the surface.)

Finally, don't lose sight of your stage images as well as your words. If you have got your structure right, and the impulse for speaking every line is properly in place, this ought to suggest a physical arrangement of elements – people, movements, objects, deeds – which has a silent poetry to it, expressing your theme. It may well be that what is visible is utterly at odds with what is being said. This is the secret to writing Dialogue which is greater than the sum of its parts.

2. WHY THIS AREA OF CRAFT IS IMPORTANT:

The following are some notes from a handout I sometimes give to students of Playwriting:

WRITING DIALOGUE
NOTES FROM FIN KENNEDY

Mastering writing dialogue can be tricky, especially for the wide variety of voices you will need to use in your work as a professional dramatist. It can be just as hard a skill to teach, and is often just a matter of endless practice. I personally found it to be like riding a bike – after years of trying and failing (it always sounded too 'written', too pre-meditated, or just too like me), one day I found I could suddenly do it and there was no looking back.

The play where it suddenly seemed to fall into place was an early fringe show I wrote called *To Be Someone*. Although it was set in London, almost all the characters were Geordies from Newcastle, a part of the country with a very distinct accent and dialect – neither of which I had any direct experience of (other than the odd episode of *Byker Grove*). The trick I found was just to go and hang around up there. The director I was developing the play for was from Newcastle, so I spent some time up there one summer, 'researching' the play, which mostly seemed to involve drinking large amounts of alcohol with various groups of Geordies. One night I went out with mostly boys, the next with mostly girls. We didn't really talk about the play as such, just about anything that came up on a night out 'on the toon', though sometimes I'd interrogate them about certain aspects of local life or culture, or ask them to repeat words or phrases they used which were specific to the area. When I got drunk enough, I'd have a go at the accent myself and they would all laugh at me.

It all felt terribly self-indulgent and the clock was ticking on my deadline. But when I got back home and set pen to paper I suddenly found all this Geordie tumbled out. The characters' voices were so clear in my head that they almost wrote themselves. Something about that immersive experience had 'locked' the energy, cadence and rhythms of young Geordies deep into my subconscious, to the extent that I found I could now call upon it to reproduce it on the page. (Plus I had a group of new Geordie friends to run the first draft past to correct any mistakes.)

I had a similar experience working on my first professionally-produced play *Protection*. The process was heavily research-led and involved interviewing and recording to tape lots of different social workers and others within the care system. Typing up their interviews, word for word, was painful and took hours, but had the same effect of somehow 'locking' their mannerisms into my mind. Those interviews became character archetypes, in terms of age, professional profile and personal background. The speech patterns that came with those categories were carried with them into the play.

The same was true of my first teenage play *Locked In*, set in an east London pirate radio station. Recording real pirate broadcasts to tape and transcribing them eventually helped me master the subcultural dialogue of east London's Caribbean and Bengali MCs and DJs (with a little help from www.urbandictionary.com and Half Moon Theatre's youth group). I was also lucky in that my other half was working in an inner city college at the time and got her students to make me a slang glossary one lesson, under the auspices of it being Sociology (which I suppose it is).

Similarly, during my time as writer-in-residence at Mulberry School in Tower Hamlets, it has been a gift to work so closely with the students in a variety of classes and after-school clubs, allowing me effortlessly to absorb the rhythms of female Bengali Muslim teenage self-expression – a group removed from me on almost every level – but for whom I now write with ease. At its best, playwriting for such diverse groups really does feel like listening to voices in your head, almost to the point of channeling something which doesn't seem to come from you at all.

I've been lucky. I have had interviewees willing to talk to me, and worked with organizations willing and able to offer me an immersive experience with very specific groups. But how do you master the wide variety of different voices in the absence of this support? This handout is an attempt to break down some of the factors that influence how a character expresses herself, and look at how they interact.

It is sometimes said that there are only two functions of dialogue in a play:

1. To advance the plot
2. To illustrate character

This may not always be the case, but I find it hard to think of scenes in any play which do neither (or any good play anyway). Obviously the ideal situation is to do both at the same time. Dialogue written merely to convey plot information on its own will quickly become bland and functional. While too much languishing in character psychology at the expense of anything happening would similarly cause a play to drag (though there are some honorable exceptions to this, see for example Jez Butterworth's *Jerusalem*). But let's look a bit more closely at what we mean by these two functions of dialogue.

We have already established in previous sessions that plots are made up of key *events*, which in turn are themselves (usually) the cumulative result of a series of smaller *actions*. Dialogue which advances the plot is therefore dialogue which in some way catalyses, reveals or is itself action – the 'doing' of something to another character. In this sense, dialogue is the vehicle by which action is conveyed, and in some cases, created.

But if there is the Protagonist advancing action then there must also be the Antagonist blocking it. This can also be made clear in the dialogue. In this sense you could argue that there are two types of plot-driven dialogue:

1. Offensive Dialogue
2. Defensive Dialogue

'Offensive' in the sense of dialogue that is part of an action pursuing an objective:

> Have you got my money then?
>
> *[Response]*
>
> Why not?
>
> *[Response]*
>
> You said it'd be today.
>
> *[Response]*
>
> Jesus, Dan, you're always bloody doing this.

'Defensive' being words that are part of a block against that action achieving its intended outcome:

> I thought we agreed next week.
>
> *[Response]*
>
> Look, things have been difficult, alright.
>
> *[Response]*
>
> Do you have to be such a dick about it?

In this sense, Type 1 dialogue means words which are part of the plot mechanism driving that scene. They can be broadly characterized as being governed by the active verbs required of dramatic action: probing, evading, persuading, obfuscating, intimidating.

Dialogue which illustrates character can be more relaxed. Its main function is more to unconsciously give away clues about the speaker, to enhance our understanding of the personalities and energies driving the action. I would say there are three 'filters' through which this type dialogue travels, and which shape its outwardly articulated form:

1. Character background
2. Character psychology
3. Character situation at that moment

'Character background' includes things like: geographical area the person was raised in (accent/dialect), class (articulacy/confidence), age (generation-specific references and tics), ethnicity and culture (specific words and phrases linked to membership of a minority group), education (articulacy – and how far some of the other factors have been 'bred out') and gender.

To extend the example, the lines written above could be tweaked to give them a Geordie inflection:

> Howay, y'got my money then?
>
> [Response]
>
> Why not, man?
>
> [Response]
>
> You said it'd be today, like.
>
> [Response]
>
> Fuck's sake Dan man, you're always bloody deeing this.

The gender question is interesting. In her book *You Just Don't Understand: Men and Women in Conversation*, linguist Deborah Tannen posits a theory. She says that men use language largely in practical terms, to discuss an issue in hand, and immediate courses of action. Women, on the other hand, use language predominantly to create an emotional connection with another speaker, and less often for practical problem-solving. Tannen argues this is why men accuse women of gossiping, and why they see little value in regular conversations with female partners or relatives unless there is 'something to say'. The reasons for speaking at all are fundamentally different between the genders.

'Character psychology' covers things like personality type, confidence, status, recent personal events, mental health and other factors affecting

6

state of mind. Thus, you could have a working class thirty-year old woman from Salford who has risen to the top of her profession as a corporate lawyer. Her background might lead you to expect her to express herself a certain way, and remnants of that will of course still be there. But her psychology, the recent past that has shaped her state of mind, indicates that this will have a particular slant due to the world she is now operating within.

Similarly, our Geordie money lender above might be inflected with a further nuance if we were to make him low status and lacking in confidence:

> Howay Dan man. Just wondering, y'know, if you had that money I lent ya?
>
> [Response]
>
> Oh right. That's a pity. D'you mind me asking, like, why and that?
>
> [Response]
>
> When d'you reckon then?
>
> [Response]
>
> Alright. Well … it's just. Y'know. I need it and that. Sometimes you do this don't ya? Not saying owt but, y'know, I'm just a bit skint and everything meself this week.

And finally 'character situation' is entirely circumstantial – and includes things like status in a certain location, or in relation to other characters, whether they are under stress or in an otherwise emotional state, what has just taken place and what is about to happen. So our working-class corporate lawyer from Salford would express herself very differently if she was:

a) in bed with a new lover;
b) speaking to a client threatening to withdraw his business;
c) in the dock on charges of embezzlement from her law firm.

Together, these factors intersect and play off each other to materially affect the words a character chooses (or doesn't choose) at any given moment in the play. Some, like accent, are permanent and unchanging (unless the play covers a very long time period). Some, like status and confidence, will change from scene to scene, depending on what is happening to the character, where and with whom.

The trick is to keep all these balls in the air at the same time. It is only by mastering the requirements of the plot, while also allowing for the influences of character background, psychology and circumstance that your drama will really fly.

3. A SIMPLE EXERCISE OR EXERCISES TO DEVELOP YOUR PLAY:

Choose two characters from your play you are working on and make some notes about the Temporary and Permanent factors which affect how they speak. For the purposes of this exercise it helps if they are as different as possible. The following prompts may be useful:

PERMANENT FACTORS

- Class
- Gender
- Age
- Region born/raised in
- Region spent most time in
- Ethnicity/cultural background
- How they learned English
- Education level
- Mental health / disability (if applicable)
- Personality type (outgoing, shy etc.)
- Articulacy (out of 10)

TEMPORARY FACTORS

- Subcultural membership (if applicable e.g. skater, emo, born again Christian)
- Emotional state at the moment
- Other characters present
- Status within scene (out of 10)
- Situation – what action has just happened, is currently happening, or is about to take place?
- Character's role within situation
- Character's role within conversation
- Location we meet them in

- Ulterior motives within scene (if known)
- Confidence level (out of 10)
- Purpose for speaking within scene
- Recent personal events
- Mental health (if applicable)

This ought to suggest two different kinds of people with detailed back stories and also generate some rough ideas for a scenario in which they meet.

Give some more thought to this scenario. Remember that the characters need to meet for a credible reason, and be given contradictory objectives which will bring them into conflict with one another. Here are some examples, you could slot your characters into one of these, or you could invent your own or use a scene from your play:

The Scene: A and B are driving in a car together when they run over and kill a cat. When they get out they see that it is their friend's cat.

A's objective: To take the cat to the friend's house and own up.

B's objective: To leave the cat where it is and not tell the friend.

■■■

The Scene: A employs B as a nanny for his/her three-year-old daughter. A has called B in for a meeting because some suspicious marks have appeared on the child's legs.

A's objective: You think B has been physically punishing your daughter. You have a powerful job and could get B investigated for all kinds of things.

B's objective: You've not been abusing the child but you are in the country illegally. Any kind of investigation and you could be deported and fined.

■■■

The Scene: A is an accountant, B is the client. A has calculated that B owes the government £10,000 in tax.

A's objective: You're a respected accountant and won't do anything dishonest or illegal.

B's objective: You want the accountant to fiddle the figures so you won't have to pay. £10,000 would ruin you and you'd have to go back to your old life of crime.

■ ■ ■

The Scene: A and B are cleaners cleaning an opulent corporate office after hours. They discover an envelope in a bin. It is stuffed with money.

A's objective: You want to keep the money and split it.

B's objective: You're scared of getting in trouble and want to report it to the boss.

■ ■ ■

The Scene: A is Editor of an important newspaper and B is a Journalist working for him / her. A tells B to do a story on a new surgical procedure that's been developed.

A's objective: Inform B that s/he will need to observe surgeons performing several operations.

B's objective: You want to make a good impression on the boss and would normally accept any assignment – but you vomit and faint at the first sign of blood. There's no way you can do this.

■ ■ ■

The Scene: A is B's boss. A has called B into his/her office to discuss some large expenses claims.

A's objective: You think B's expenses are fraudulent and s/he has forged some receipts.

B's objective: You forged the receipts because you think you're under-paid, but you can't say that outright. Instead you feign anger that A is questioning your professional integrity

Note that the most useful scenarios all contain some circumstantial information and a pre-existing relationship between the characters. Try to keep this in any scenarios you invent. 'Strangers on a park bench' is unlikely to generate much of interest.

EXERCISE

You now have two characters with personalities and histories and an idea for a scenario which will bring them into conflict and require them to speak.

If you have an idea of their names, use these, otherwise just call them A and B for now (however it is important to know if they are male or female).

Write ten lines of the scene you have chosen. Check how they are speaking and if it fits with everything you know about who they are and what they want. If it doesn't, go back and fix their lines so that it does.

When you're happy, write another ten lines.

Then another.

Then another.

Then do the permanent and temporary factors for the rest of your characters in your play.

You are then ready to write the rest of your play.

Write the first draft of your play.

Good luck!

LESSON PLAN SEVEN
THEATRICALITY

BY STEVE WINTER, DIRECTOR OF THE KEVIN SPACEY FOUNDATION

I. FOCUS:

This lesson plan is focused on Theatricality. I have defined it here, in a theatre-making context, as: *Creating an emotional reaction that draws focus.* Theatricality is also to do with stage directions and the visual images and feelings you create.

2. WHY THIS AREA OF CRAFT IS IMPORTANT:

Theatricality is important because it builds meaning into a production; it allows for collaboration within every area of the theatre-making process and allows you to enhance your words and vision.

7

Some of the following exercises assume you're working with other writers where exploration around theatricality can be collaborative and supportive but you can also complete them on your own or find a friend or fellow writer to work with if you are working on your own.

3. A SIMPLE EXERCISE OR EXERCISES TO DEVELOP YOUR PLAY:

EXERCISE 1: STAGE DIRECTIONS

Stage directions are the playwright's only say in the visual theatricality of their play, before the interpretations of the creative team during the rehearsal process. You will likely have written several into your current play draft. However, it's important to strike a balance as leading the mood of every scene can leave the creative team with little room to play. Conversely not saying enough can leave the creative team confused.

The following is my key advice:

- Be consistent – Go through your script and ensure all of your stage directions are laid out consistently. I prefer in bold and in brackets but some people use italics. Consistency applies for both scene setting directions and directions in speeches.
- Be open – Go through your script and edit out directions that may be too cumbersome or unachievable or too directive.

- Be clear – Go through your script and ensure what you're suggesting makes sense and relates to the scene or speech you're referring to.

EXERCISE 2:

Prepare a version of your script without stage directions. Then partner with a fellow writer who will have done the same. Swap scripts and read twice through.

In the second read circle/underline scenes that you have an emotional reaction to i.e. you laugh; feel fearful, tense, intrigued etc. adding notes or comments as you do so. This is your theatricality list.

Come together as a pair and compare and contrast your scripts both *with* the stage directions and *without* the stage directions. Discuss what has and has not had an emotional affect; this will be useful as you begin your next draft.

If you are working on your own, complete the above exercise by removing the stage directions then circling yourself what you have an emotional reaction to then analyzing whether you need to revise stage directions to bring these moments out more clearly.

In both cases, revise your stage directions as needed to bring out these moments more clearly.

EXERCISE 3: ASSETS

ACTORS

A good creative team will always be respectful to the playwright by executing the theatricality already written into the page but a diverse company of actors is theatrical in itself. So consider whom you would like in your piece. Does it require a great physical performer, comedian, 'leading man' or someone of a certain age? Can you get them in to read a draft and improvise with you?

PROPS/SET

Props and set that act as a visual metaphor are particularly theatrical or props that are transformed into multiple uses. So assuming you know where it's going to be staged (for example if you are going to stage your plays at your school or University) conduct a recce. What props and set are in the building, what local businesses could lend you something; who could make something for you? If you don't know where it is going to be staged, ask yourself the same question – how could you best use props and set as a visual metaphor in your play?

Consider your audience and the visual affect you're aiming for when they arrive in the space. Is the stage set hidden or in view? How important is it that they know the period? How important is the element of surprise? Can you use Front of House to sign post entry into the space, for example by doing something in the lobby or similar?

Revise your stage directions based on the above as useful.

4. FINAL ADVICE

Creating theatricality is rewarding and fun, particularly in a big group. It's also often aligned with a certain style or period. However, it shouldn't exclude other forms such as 'realism' or 'kitchen sink' but rather should complement them.

And finally having worked with playwrights for many years most write theatricality into their script in the hope that it will inspire the creative team working on it offering clarity to the story and permission to play. So let that be your guiding instinct overall.

LESSON PLAN EIGHT
REWRITING

BY CAROLINE JESTER, DRAMATURG AND AUTHOR OF *PLAYWRITING ACROSS THE CURRICULUM* AND *FIFTY PLAYWRIGHTS ON THEIR CRAFT*

I. FOCUS:

Congratulations, you've written your play. So why is there another lesson plan? Isn't it time to hand the play over to a director, get the actors booked and stage the play?

This lesson plan will explore rewriting, which is the stage where a writer often begins to unearth the secrets that are in the script that they didn't even realize were there. The aim of this lesson plan is to provide the writer with new ideas for their play, to facilitate the rewriting process.

We will explore how the collaborative nature of theatre can also be applied to the process of rewriting. We will take the first draft of the play and work together to establish what works well and what needs more research and/or rewriting. We will see if the writer's intentions for the play are coming through in the text by examining scenes within the play. We will see if the characters' objectives are clear and if the obstacles that are placed in front of them serve to push the action forward. We'll see if the timeframe and structure supports the narrative and if the locations the characters inhabit support the dramatic action.

Each writer will finish with a list of questions and ideas that they can apply to their script. This will be achieved by inhabiting different 'roles' within the craft of dramatic writing; the playwright, the actor and the dramaturg. We shall explore a situation similar to the professional playwright's 'workshop phase' – a stage in new writing development where actors read through an early draft of the script with the purpose of developing the play, not judging the material as a finished piece.

2. WHY THIS AREA OF CRAFT IS IMPORTANT:

The play is written and the writer is confident that it will be easily translatable to the creative team; the actors, director, producer, designer and ultimately the audience.

There are many names for this first draft, and many unpopular with writers, but unless it is one of those rare gems that need little reworking this will be in a raw state. It can be disheartening if a writer hands their play over to others to read and they come back with a list of questions that the writer believed were clearly answered through the characters' actions within their play.

Reflective practice is a crucial skill a writer needs to develop to be able to push their work to the next level by rewriting, rewriting and a bit more rewriting. To ensure their brilliant idea, the one that made them sit at the desk typing away for hours when they could have been partaking in other more social activities, does what they expected it to do. It's all too easy to send that first draft off before reflecting on whether those scenes that you thought were brilliant writing, even though they feel out of character with the action of the play, are actually needed. Is that monologue half way through pushing the story forward or being used as a mouth piece for the writer's ideas rather than their characters? Can the writer really introduce ten new characters in the penultimate scene because they feel this makes it easier for the protagonist to get that backstory in that wasn't realized at the beginning of the play? Isn't this functional rather than active, something no one will really notice, will they…

These are the things you want to iron out of your script before you send it off to producers. It takes skill to look at your play from this critical angle but once you develop this, it will only serve to support your play and future writing. Your characters will begin to take on a life of their own that is separate from your initial intention. The play will be alive, and it is this that will make your work stand out.

Rewriting is exploring the work in progress and being open to many changes along the way. Don't be afraid of this stage because the deeper you dig, the more discoveries you'll make along the way, not only about the play you're writing now, but about you as a writer.

3. A SIMPLE EXERCISE OR EXERCISES TO DEVELOP YOUR PLAY:

GROUP PREPARATION

We will be working in groups. If you are working with a large class you might want to break this into smaller groups once you have established the principles. If you are writing on your own, now is the time to gather fellow students or a group of friends together. Each member of the group will change roles throughout the exercise and be the writer, actor and dramaturg. This will help the writers see plays from three different perspectives, fostering a more critical outlook on their own plays.

The writer casts the play from other members of the group, they become the actors. The rest of the group will act as 'dramaturgs'. A dramaturg in this instance is someone who will ask questions about the play to help push the writer into thinking more deeply about their work, both the subject matter and its mechanics. What the dramaturgs are not there to do is to suggest 'better' ways of writing the play.

Once the play has been cast by the writer each 'actor' will be given a copy of the script. If the scripts are short and time permits read the whole play but if time is limited and it is a full length piece then this exercise can work by using a single scene or scenes from the play. The scenes do not have to be taken chronologically and it is a useful exercise to choose a scene or section that isn't quite working rather than using this as an exercise to present a 'polished' section. The aim of the exercise is to enable the writer to find a route into reworking the play rather than staging the text.

It is useful to give a time limit on each scene or extract as this can help facilitate an understanding of what can be achieved in terms of action within a play in a certain timeframe.

So we're ready to go. We've got the writer, the actors and the dramaturgs. And the first draft…

The writer can give a brief introduction to the characters to help the actors understand them but they are not allowed to give an introduction to the play. For example they can say things like:

Jack 28, an environment agency worker

Naylah, 40 a secondary school teacher

Tess, 14 and loves to row

What we don't want is an introduction that tries to explain what the whole play is about and the relationships between characters, therefore 'planting' ideas for reactions from the 'dramaturgs'. We're aiming to see what is already in the play. We want to see what it shows us through the dramatic action.

ONE THING I LIKED ABOUT THE SCENE

The actors now read the scene to everyone. Here's an example of a précis of the action within a scene:

> Naylah is refusing to evacuate her flat, which is flooded from the river near her home that has burst its banks. She won't leave until someone comes with boxes to put her two cats in. Jack needs to get around all the other houses and doesn't have time for this. Evacuate means evacuate. Tess appears on her own with a cat box. How did she get down the street on her own when all the boats are in use by the rescue teams? Where did she find this boat?

All the dramaturgs must say one thing they liked about the play or scene. There are no rules or restrictions to apply here and there can be repetition. For example:

> I liked the way Tess appeared in a boat on her own.

> I liked the fact that Naylah wouldn't leave the flat without her cats.

The only rule is that all of the dramaturgs must say something. The writer will write these down but will not respond. Once all the dramaturgs have responded the writer will now have a list of things that people like about their play. This might connect with the writer's intention or provide insight into things and characters an audience is intrigued by. The writer might be surprised if they thought the play was about one character's story and everyone is more intrigued by another character. This can unlock new ideas and connections that hadn't previously been explored.

A QUESTION

Now we're going to dig deeper and see if we can help the writer understand what isn't clear about the scene. The dramaturgs will now all:

> Ask one question about the play/scene they have heard.

Once again the writer cannot respond and must write the questions down. If the writer does start to answer the questions, because this is an instinctive response when questioned, remind the writer that they are being provided with questions to reflect on for the rewriting process. If they are explaining the play then it might also be due to lack of clarity in the script. An area to rewrite….

It does not matter if the dramaturgs repeat things they liked from the previous exercise because this serves to indicate to the writer what an audience might respond well to. The questions about the play/scene, however, have a few rules. They cannot be subjective such as:

I didn't like the way Jack was moaning, I'd have written the scene completely differently.

It doesn't make any sense that Tess appears from nowhere.

Naylah wouldn't stay in her flat. It's too unbelievable.

What we are looking for here instead of opinions are questions that explore the scenes that have been read. If theatre is something that happens in the present then we are dealing with the specifics of any given moment to generate the action. We're looking for questions about what is happening in the scene to provide the writer with a new set of keys to open doors within their play that were previously locked to them. By focusing on specific questions that relate to the scene we have heard we can begin to unearth things that might need exploring in the rewrites.

For example if it's unclear why a character is doing something in a scene, if it doesn't feel like they would be doing what they are doing then a way to explore this could be through questions such as:

Where has Tess just come from?

Has she got her parents' permission to rescue people?

Is Tess trying to rescue other people or just Naylah?

By understanding where the characters have just come from immediately prior to the scene you begin to explore how and why they are behaving the way they do. If they're agitated this could be because of a previous encounter that was stressful that is making their behavior in this scene unusual. We don't want this information through exposition but through the subtext that is generated by the dramatic action, what they are doing in that moment. This can be developed into:

What is Jack's objective in the scene?

Does Jack really want to help Naylah leave her flat?

Has Tess stolen the boat?

We start to see what's happening in the scene and subsequently the characters' journeys within the wider play. If we develop this into seeing what stops them getting what they want, their obstacles, we can see if there is conflict driving the scene forward.

Is Naylah preventing Jack from rescuing other residents?

Is Tess beneficial to Jack's rescue mission or another problem because she's now another person to evacuate?

Questions about the location and environment can help facilitate the writer's understanding of how characters behave and is often something that isn't thought about fully in a first draft. If we look at location as active, a character in itself then this can help the characters too. The questions are often very simple:

Does the scene happen outside the door to Naylah's flat?

If we're inside her flat then in which room? Be specific.

How deep is the water and how has this affected the environment within the flat?

Is she standing on tables holding her animals?

If the scene is in a public space then who else is there?

Has the writer explored structure and timeframe fully? Does this support the narrative they want to tell? The questions do not have to be complicated to ignite a writer's understanding of choices they are making.

What time of day is it?

Will the play take place over twenty-four hours or three years?

Will the play take place in real time?

This helps to think about the emotional journeys of the characters and if the key events within the play are placed correctly to achieve the writer's intention. If the play takes place over three years then it will more than likely not be a highly charged emotional drama or have an imminent sense of urgency.

AN ACTOR'S RESPONSE

Now let's turn to the actors. They will ask one question each but the rule here is that it has to be a question that is related to the character and/or the relationships between the characters they were reading. For example:

How long has Jack been working for the environment agency?

Is Naylah Tess's teacher?

If Naylah is Tess's teacher how well do they get on in class?

When did Tess become interested in rowing?

If an actor says something like:

I don't think Tess would shout at her teacher

try to explore this further by turning it into a question with reference to the scene such as:

Has Tess ever shouted at her teacher Naylah before?

This simple question opens up the characters' histories and the subtext as well as thinking how an actor would play this by understanding what is happening in this moment. The writer does not answer the questions but writes them down.

THREE LISTS

The writer will now have three lists:

1. The first list will give the writer an idea of what an audience is connecting with through what they immediately liked about the play.
2. The second list will contain questions about the scene/play that the writer can answer after they have reflected on them.
3. The third list might be similar to the second list but it should contain more specific questions about characters and their relationships.

The process will be repeated for each play and the roles will be swapped until everyone has inhabited the skin of the writer, actor and dramaturg.

SITTING DOWN TO REWRITE ALONE

The writer can become overwhelmed with all this feedback. This then is another crucial stage in learning to trust your own voice. If a question feels unhelpful then strike it from the list. You've been writing your play and know more about it than anyone else and if it feels out of sync with the play then do not become fixated on answering all the questions. If there is repetition, however, then pay attention to the question because there might be something crucial here that could push the narrative forward or provide insight into a missing link. Once you have reflected on the questions from the group try to look at each scene within your play and answer the following questions:

What does each character want at the beginning of the scene?

What stops each character achieving what they want in the scene?

Is the location of the scene being used effectively by the characters or should they be more aware of their environment?

What happens in the scene?

What has changed for each character by the end of the scene?

If we look at each scene as a small unit of action within the whole play then something must happen. If a scene does not work then it is often because the writer feels we need a scene that tells an audience something, is expositional, rather than allowing the characters to show us through dramatic action. The play is a constellation of characters in a slice of life chosen to explore something a writer feels needs telling. The writer chooses carefully by being specific about what is needed to achieve this.

So what's the play about then?

Finally in one sentence write what the play is about.

Has this changed from when you started writing the play?

It may change again as you begin rewriting but it's a useful sentence to put above your laptop and remind yourself what you're trying to achieve and keep focused. The aim of rewriting is to turn the raw material from the first draft into a focused and specific piece of dramatic writing that would have answered some of the questions the dramaturgs thought were important in the first draft so it's ready to be staged.

4. FINAL ADVICE

The aim of these exercises is not to follow the advice of another and rewrite your play to answer all the questions but to see what is already there in your work. To help develop reflective practice.

Playwriting is ultimately collaborative, because it is written for others to play and for an audience to be witness to. What we're hoping to explore here is applying the collaborative process to the writing stage in the form of seeing how the work translates before the audience comes in so we can sharpen the text and narrative.

As writers, though, your role is to be discerning at all stages. If the feedback doesn't feel right, then reflect on this but be ready to disregard it. This is part of the rewriting process, you understanding your material more and taking charge of it as it changes along the way. We want to see work that has a strong authorial voice on our stages and the process of rewriting is ultimately about you as the writer, asserting your voice through work that resonates with your audience.

8

LESSON PLAN NINE
STAGING YOUR WORK

BY CAROLINE HORTON, WRITER, PERFORMER, DIRECTOR
AND MENTOR NOMINATED BY THE BUSH THEATRE

I. FOCUS:

This lesson looks at how to stage your work once your play is written. There are many different ways of going about this of course, and here I'll simply be offering some options and tips based on my experiences.

I'll be focusing on producing the show yourself (the DIY approach), as this is where my experience lies. I have always collaborated with and been supported by venues and producers however, so there is definitely cross-over with the approach that seeks venues/producers who might be interested in producing your play themselves.

The objective of this lesson plan is to break down the task of staging your work into some manageable steps. These include possible interim stages such as setting up a play-reading or workshopping the play with actors and a director.

2. WHY THIS AREA OF BUSINESS IS IMPORTANT:

Until I hear a play out loud, and watch performers play with the text in a space, I don't properly understand what it is I'm writing. A reading or workshop will immediately offer lots of information about what needs looking at in the next draft. They can be great opportunities to get fresh eyes and ears on the piece and gather valuable feedback. This is daunting – suddenly these characters and words that have been in your head for months, are handed to other people and received by an audience. But it's exciting too and a brilliant tool for the development of the piece.

From a business point of view, readings or work-in-progress performances are a way for people to get to know your work; an opportunity to meet future collaborators (directors, designers, actors, theatre programmers or producers) who might be interested in working with you at a later date. A note of caution, though: think carefully about the best point at which to invite decision-makers and stakeholders. The very first reading might be better as a learning experience for your benefit than as a shop window for theirs.

Staging a piece is a collaboration and the sooner the creative team starts coming together, the greater the opportunity to build strong relationships and truly explore the show's possibilities together. I've always found it important to build a tight team around a piece, who can support it through its development, which inevitably will have its rocky moments.

3. A SIMPLE EXERCISE OR EXERCISES USING THIS BUSINESS ELEMENT TO DEVELOP YOUR PLAY:

In getting your script from the page to a full-production, there are some stages along the way that might be useful to you:

- set up a play reading
- workshop the play or a few scenes from the play
- present short work-in-progress performances to an audience

TIPS:

1. Here are some things to consider when setting up a play-reading:

– **Venue** – This could be a living room of course, but if you want to invite people you don't know, look into finding a space to rent or if you have a relationship with a local theatre, they might let you use one of their spaces. It's always worth approaching a theatre whose programme you think resonates with your piece about the possibility of offering you space for a reading – it might be a way of starting a conversation with them.

– **Director** – Start having conversations with potential directors as early as you can. Ask around for suggestions and recommendations. Is there someone whose work you've seen and admired that you could have a coffee with about your piece? Look out in theatre programmes for assistant directors too – they might be looking to get their teeth into something for themselves.

You could ask them to help you prepare for the reading with the performers, or perhaps inviting them to the reading is the start of your conversation with them. (I'd also be inclined to meet with or invite possible designers along too – make a note of designers from brilliant pieces you've loved.)

9

– **Actors** – Who do you want to be involved? Are there specific skills you need such as an actor who can sing? Think about people you know or again ask around for suggestions. Are there performers you've seen who you could approach? Talk to your director about suggestions too. If you're at the point where there's no funding attached to the project, be clear about this – a reading is a relatively small commitment if you're asking people to work for free but talk with performers about your long-term plans for the piece (who you're talking to, where you hope to stage the show, funding plans etc.). In my experience it's great to build your team as early as you can – then everyone develops a genuine attachment and investment in the production.

– **Audience** – Invite people to the reading. I'd suggest this is made up of some people you know and some you don't. You want supportive friends there but also some people you don't know, who will worry less about being honest. If it's happening in a theatre, perhaps they would be interested in asking particular groups along (e.g. emerging artists or associates).

Also, it's a good moment to invite anyone useful industry-wise along – do this well in advance and be clear about what the piece is, at what stage and how long the reading will be. These might be independent producers whose work resonates with your own, artistic directors/producers/literary managers from venues that you have relationships with or that produce work that would seem a good fit for your piece. Be sure to do your research so people don't feel they are getting blanket impersonal emails, show you know what they do and the sort of work they're involved in.

– **Feedback** – It's useful to provide a simple handout with a bit of info about you and your work, the play itself, what you want to learn from this reading and where you hope to go with it next. Include the names of the creatives you're working with (actors/director/designer etc.) and your contact details. For me, an informal Q&A after the reading has always been the most helpful way to get interesting/useful feedback but I always also offer tear-off forms at the bottom of the free handout for written feedback and for people to leave their email so you can inform them of future plans for the piece.

2. Here are some things to consider when workshopping the play/or an extract:

As a theatre maker from a performing and devising background, workshopping text is integral to my process. I devise with a team in the room and then go away and write, before returning once more to the devising room.

How much workshopping you can do depends on budget, time and your preferred process.

When I have a draft that needs new eyes on it and to be experimented with, I'll start with a reading with the director, performers (one of whom is usually me!) and any more of the creative team who are involved and available. We'll then immediately begin to workshop it – roughly trying out scenes up on our feet. I like a rehearsal room where everyone can chip in – especially at this stage – though this depends on a room of good listeners!

Warming up: I'm often tempted to just dive into the text but playing complicity games and games to encourage trust, spontaneity and playfulness can transform the rather daunting experience of workshopping a new piece.

For me, workshopping tends to be a closed room – just the team present. A safe place for experimenting, taking risks and getting it wrong.

Often after reading a scene a few times, I find it useful to take away the text and just have the performers improvise the scene. Doing this, we can look for what the essential game or dynamic is beyond the specific words I've written.

Adding in a physical game can open up new dimensions for a scene. For example, a scene I was workshopping recently involved a character getting increasingly ecstatic and exhausted. The director added in a physical exercise routine for the performer, in which she had to keep going no matter what, while the other character had to try different tactics to snap her out of it. The director had hit upon the essential dynamic and given the scene a hilarious visual journey and I realized I could lose about half the text!

As you explore the text in the workshop, keep in mind whether the scene excites you? Is it necessary? Is there something missing? Is it too long? (Probably!) Is it clear? Am I bored at points? Am I saying things that are already clear in the visual storytelling of the piece?

Then come away and discuss the overall structure and movement of the piece with the director and plan your next moves. Perhaps it's another rewrite or do you want to find an opportunity to perform a short extract for an audience to discover more?

3. Staging a production yourself

If you decide to stage the production yourself, rather than submitting your script to theatres, these exercises will help you clarify your aims and create a plan with manageable, concrete tasks to set you on your way.

EXERCISE PART 1:

Thirty minutes

Spend five minutes under each heading speed-writing about your vision for the production. Don't think too much – just write.

What	What is your end goal and what are the stages leading to a full production?
Why	Write a blurb. This forces you to identify and start being able to communicate what is special about your show; why people should be interested in funding/supporting/coming to see it.
Who	Write down who is involved and identify who you still need to find to complete the team.
Where	Write down all the theatres and festivals that might be interested in your show – whether from a programming point of view or offering you support along the way.

When	Write a rough timeline for getting your production on (starting from now).
How	How are you going to fund it? What are your funding options? What do you need in place to apply for funding?

An Example (don't worry if you haven't got this much detail in yours).

A plan for new play 'Civil'

WHAT

Rehearse and stage full production of 'Civil' to premiere at Edinburgh Fringe Festival in 2017 with a view to touring UK in Spring 2018.

WHY

Exciting new show drawing on personal and family experience of pursuing cases through the civil court in the face of the government cuts to legal aid. Irreverent; great night out; playful.

Live music, easily tourable – small cast and set.

A showcase for me as a writer.

An important story about legal-aid cuts – touches on this live political issue through a personal story showing us the real-life effects of government cuts. Draws on interviews in research period. Political with a small 'p'.

The form is exciting, immediate.

Uses funny childhood film footage, live music. There's a direct audience relationship.

WHO

Producer? Might need to self-produce. But research those making work you love and invite producers to previews (don't forget to think about assistant producers).

Director – already agreed.

One other performer and another performer/musician – find recommendations – see work and invite performers you like to meet with you.

Designer – make a list from shows you've been excited by.

Production Manager – ask around for suggestions – write a rough job spec e.g. do they need some lighting design skills.

Lighting designer? Depending on budget – research who companies you admire have worked with.

Dramaturge? Depending on budget – be clear how much time you're asking for. Are they in the room with you or just reading drafts?

WHERE

Process split between Birmingham and London. Rehearsals with supporting venue. Approach BAC? mac Birmingham?

A preview run somewhere before Edinburgh? Or a set of work-in-progress shows at different venues. Old Red Lion, Hen and Chickens? Brighton Fringe (which venues?) Theatre 503, Ovalhouse?

Edinburgh Fringe (Pleasance. Summerhall, Forest Fringe, Assembly, Gilded Balloon, Underbelly, Zoo)

Possible tour venues to invite to Edinburgh:

Arcola, South Street, Reading, mac Birmingham, Birmingham Rep, Exeter Bike Shed, Derby Theatre (Departure Lounge), Pulse (New Wolsey Theatre), Battersea Arts Centre, Cambridge Junction, Quarterhouse Folkestone, Liverpool Unity, Warwick Arts Centre.

9

WHEN

Reading and Workshop day in one month's time. Mid-March 16.

Re-writes based on what I learnt – allow two weeks. Complete end of March.

Finalize team, send out final draft, team meeting to discuss plan for staging the piece. April 16

Research funding possibilities (including deadlines) and ask for support from venues and set up penciled performance dates. April 16.

Apply for funding. Deadline for submission end of May 16 (unless funds have particular deadlines).

Results from funding. If unsuccessful go back to researching funding phase – there's always a plan B - if successful continue with plan.

Production meeting – whole team, logistics, going over budgets.

Design meeting

Rehearsals two weeks September 16

Week gap for rewrites

Invite industry to the run a month before.

Rehearsals four weeks Oct/Nov 16

Short preview run at fringe theatre one week November/December 16

Apply to Edinburgh festival Jan 17

Invite industry, press, and potential touring venues

Re-rehearse two weeks July 17

Four week run at Edinburgh festival 2017

Book tour for Spring 2018

HOW

List of potential funding bodies to apply to. Research!

Approach theatres for small commissions.

Crowd-funding campaign – think up unusual, exciting rewards.

Fundraising event? Brainstorm – talk to people who've done this.

Apply to Arts Council for a small grants for the arts award. Read guidelines online thoroughly and call them for advice if necessary. Talk to people who've had successful grants – maybe ask to read one?

Apply to other trusts and funds e.g. Kevin Spacey Foundation – research more.

EXERCISE PART 2:

Fifteen minutes

Create a set of ten concrete action points for the next two weeks:

Example

1. Start assembling team: write eight emails to potential collaborators suggesting meeting up about the project
2. Build support for my arts council application (I'll need some seed funding and support in kind). Email my contact at my local theatre to set up a meeting to discuss the idea and my plan for the production.

3. Read Arts Council application guidelines on website (NB Arts Council doesn't fund performances outside England – so Edinburgh's out)

4. Email a friend who has written a successful Arts Council application to pick their brains and see if I can read it.

5. Email five possible supporting venues to ask for space to hold a play reading.

6. Write a list of other potential funding bodies/trusts to apply to and make a note of deadlines.

7. Draw up a very rough budget for the development of the piece – is there someone you could ask for a sample budget to use as a template?

8. Collect ten examples of theatre marketing you like – look at the images and blurbs and have a go at outlining the design and blurb for your own production. Write five emails to print designers for quotes.

9. Research deadlines for festivals e.g. Departure Lounge Derby, Edinburgh, and Brighton Fringe. Make a list.

10. Write a first bad draft of an arts council application and talk it through with someone.

Once your two weeks are up, see how far along you got and write yourself a new set of action points for the next two weeks.

4. FINAL ADVICE:

Ask for help and advice – people are generally happy to help. Make sure you thank them properly and credit them where you can and they'll help you again.

Feedback – be as open as you can be to feedback, then go away and think it through and see if it needs "translating" a bit to become helpful to you. For example, someone might be pointing to a section of the play that isn't working yet but their specific suggestion might not be helpful for your piece – so it's up to you to find your own solutions to the problem they've helped identify.

See as much work as you can and have conversations with other artists and companies – there's a wealth of information out there and people are generally willing to share their expertise.

LESSON PLAN TEN
FINAL ADVICE

BY LUCY KERBEL, FOUNDER AND DIRECTOR OF TONIC THEATRE
AND THE PLATFORM PROJECT FOR WRITING FOR YOUNG AUDIENCES

I. FOCUS:

The exercise in this lesson plan encourages you to reflect on how you can take steps forward in your professional life as a writer. Being a professional writer means that part or all of the money you earn comes from the writing you do. Becoming a professional writer relies not just on you being talented. It's also down to you being organized, self-disciplined, understanding the industry you're walking into, and giving yourself the best possible opportunity to do well.

Of course, not all people who write do it professionally: many do it simply because they enjoy it, not because they want to make a living from it. You may feel you want to make writing your job, or you may want it to be something you do in your spare time. Either way, the exercise in this lesson plan should be helpful in encouraging you to think about *why* you're writing, *who* you want to reach with it, and *how*.

2. WHY THIS AREA OF BUSINESS IS IMPORTANT:

If you're writing for the stage, you'll want an audience for your work. To stand the best chance of your scripts being performed before the public (rather than remaining on your computer!), you'll need to be organized and dedicated to making this happen. Generally writers have to split their focus between two things: getting their heads down and writing the plays they want to, and getting their work 'out there' so it stands the best possible chance of being staged. This is a constant balancing act for writers: you could be the most brilliant writer, but if no one knows your work exists it's unlikely to ever get on stage. But being entirely preoccupied with building your career, to the exclusion of giving the time to your writing that it needs, may mean you never develop as far as you could as a writer.

---

3. A SIMPLE EXERCISE OR EXERCISES USING THIS BUSINESS ELEMENT TO DEVELOP YOUR PLAY:

Exercise: SWOT analysis

This is an exercise that originally comes from the business world, but is also really useful for writers and all types of creative people. It can help you reflect on where you'd like to go professionally and how you can best focus your energies to do that.

'SWOT' is an acronym. It stands for:

S = STRENGTHS

W = WEAKNESSES

O = OPPORTUNITIES

T = THREATS

First of all, in a notebook or on a blank piece of paper, draw four columns. Then at the top of each column write 'strengths', 'weaknesses', 'opportunities', 'threats'. Then think about yourself at this moment in time and fill in each column about where you feel you are at right now in regards to your writing, and your writing career.

Try not to take too long over completing the columns – give yourself no more than ten minutes to get through all four. As you write, try not to censor yourself or worry about 'getting it wrong'; just scribble down anything that comes into your head whether or not it feels important. One of the aims of this exercise is to bring things to the front of your brain you might not previously have been aware of. So work fast and write down everything that pops into your head.

As you go, ask yourself questions such as:

STRENGTHS

What am I good at?

What is interesting about my writing?

Where am I particularly confident?

What about me and my writing sets me apart from others?

What are the accolades, awards, or recognition my writing has won in the past?

WEAKNESSES

Where do I lack experience?

What have I yet to learn?

What traits do I have that might prevent me doing my best work?

In what areas do I lack confidence?

Where are the gaps in my knowledge or understanding?

OPPORTUNITIES

Who are the people who might want to work with me to stage my work e.g. directors, actors?

What are the playwriting awards or schemes I could apply for?

What are the places I could go to learn more about writing?

What resources exist that could help me to get my head down and focus on my writing?

Who are the people I could ask for advice about next steps?

THREATS

Who is my competition?

Who could I let stop me from doing my writing?

What could reduce how much time I get to spend writing?

What are the other commitments I have in my life that could take my focus away?

What are the practical barriers to me taking the next steps as a writer?

As a rule, 'strengths' and 'weaknesses' are about you and relate to things you can largely control or have an impact on (for instance, a personal weakness that may prevent you writing as much as you'd like is having a tendency to let your attention wander). 'Opportunities' and 'threats' are about the outside world; they're about things going on around you which may be outside your immediate control (for instance a threat to you writing as much as you'd like is recognizing you don't have much time to write because you're juggling three jobs to pay your rent).

A person's completed SWOT analysis might look something like this:

STRENGTHS

I'm good at talking to people about my work and feel quite comfortable 'selling' myself to them.

I was shortlisted for a playwriting award and can put that on my CV.

I have an interest in producing so could maybe look into putting some of my own work on.

WEAKNESSES

I don't really understand how theatres make decisions about which plays they select; I don't really know what they're looking for.

I find far too many excuses not to do my writing, especially if I've hit a tricky moment in the writing process.

I've written short pieces but wouldn't feel confident tackling a full-length piece.

OPPORTUNITIES

My local theatre is running some playwriting sessions – maybe I should join those.

There are lots of playwriting awards – I could apply to some of them.

I have friends who act – they might be happy to help me develop some of my scripts further.

THREATS

My house is really noisy and it's hard to focus when I try to write there.

The hours I work make it difficult to find the time to write.

My friends laugh at me for wanting to be a writer and this affects my confidence.

Once you've filled in all four columns, take some time to reflect back on what you've written. In particular, make a note of anything that surprises you about what you've written, or anything that you find interesting. Don't speed through this part of the process – the point of this exercise is that you really *think* about where you are at the moment. So make yourself a cup of tea, find yourself somewhere quiet to drink it where you won't get interrupted, and really take your time to ponder over what you've just written.

Once you've done that, the next step is to think about what you want to prioritize in response to what you found yourself writing – how can you build on your strengths and capitalize on opportunities? How can you address your weaknesses and as far as possible mitigate the threats you face? Remember you can't address everything at once and some things will take longer than others. So maybe pick between three and six things you want to focus on first, then work out an action and give yourself a timeframe for moving forward in regards to it. For instance:

WHAT I WROTE ON MY SWOT ANALYSIS:

"My house is really noisy and it's hard to focus when I try to write there"

Action:

Investigate what quiet, calm spaces there are in my local area to write e.g. libraries and coffee shops.

Timeframe:

One month. Given that I write at weekends, I'll try writing in a different location (not at home!) for the next four weekends and see if I find my focus improves in any of them.

WHAT I WROTE ON MY SWOT ANALYSIS:

"I don't really understand how theatres make decisions about which plays they select; I don't really know what they're looking for"

Action:

Spend some time doing online research into different theatres; I'll really look at what they say about themselves and their artistic vision on their websites, what kind of work they produce, I'll read reviews of plays they've staged and try to work out whether my plays fit with the kind of work they seem interested in staging.

Timeframe:

Six months. I'll carve out thirty minutes a week to do this and will keep notes so I don't forget what I'm learning as I go.

One you've set tasks and timeframes for yourself, make sure you stick to them! Then repeat the SWOT analysis every six months or so – it'll be interesting to see where you're making progress and where you need to make yourself work harder.

4. FINAL ADVICE:

As a writer, or in any creative activity, taking time to be self-reflective is crucial. Question yourself, examine where you're doing well, and be honest with yourself about where you could be doing better. Recognize that setting aside time to do this is a necessity, not a luxury!

10

PART TWO
THE WINNING WORK

THE STUDENT GUIDE TO BEING A STUDENT IN THE UK

BY MIRIAM BATTYE, MONIQUE GERAGTHY, TITILOLA IGE,
MUFARO MAKUBIKA AND VEE TAMES;
CURATED AND GUIDED BY JENNIFER TUCKETT

SECTIONS/CHARACTERS

LUCY THE GUIDE BY JENNIFER TUCKETT
LUCY, The Guide

OLD ME, NEW ME BY TITILOLA IGE
ME, *female*

THE OTHER SIDE BY VEE TAMES
AYESHA, *female*

NUMBERS BY MIRIAM BATTYE
MEG, *female*

REFUND BY MUFARO MAKUBIKA
STUDENT, *male*

THE FUTURE OF EDUCATION BY MONIQUE GERAGHTY

FUTURE STUDENT, *can be played by a male or female actor*

The play is a promenade play, which can be performed anywhere
from school or University classrooms to potentially different
sections of the same room or theatre if you only have one space.

SCENE ONE

LUCY, aged twenty-one, enters. She is carrying a clipboard.

LUCY: Hello and welcome to The Student Guide to Being a Student in the UK.

My name is Lucy and I am going to be your guide today.

And I am very excited that you are here because we are going to vote on whether it is important to be a student in the UK today or not.

Which is a very important issue, as I'm sure you know.

And, if you don't, I'm going to give you a tour of a few different students' ideas to help you decide.

These students have been selected from all over the UK to take part in our tour, which is going to be very exciting, I promise.

But before we begin here are a few rules:

She refers to her clipboard.

Number One: it is important you stay with the group at all times, do not stray away from the group or you may disappear into the midsts of the educational system and never be seen again. I'm not joking. This has occurred.

Number Two: do not run, do not dance, do not hop. Proceed with seriousness and cautiousness at all times. This is a serious subject.

And finally

Number Three: listen to my advice. This is very important, because I am a student and being your guide is counting towards my marks and I really need to do well on this, thank you.

She finishes with her clipboard.

And, so, on that note, let's begin the tour of The Student Guide to Being a Student in the UK.....

Follow me.

LUCY leads them to the first room.

SCENE TWO: OLD ME/NEW ME BY TITILOLA IGE

Chairs lined up in two rows like a bus. She sits on the second row.

Me: Old Me.

Sweaty. Always walking fast. Constantly listening to other people's conversations on the bus.

Constantly.

> *Moves to a different seat. She listens to other people's conversations.*

Other people's lives were much, much more interesting than my own. I lived for hearing stories such as 'Girl Chewing Gum Really Hard Then Twisting It Round Her Finger' tells 'Other Girl With Too Much Gel in Her Hair That it Looks Like Dandruff' – about something that would mean absolutely nothing to them – would be absolutely insignificant – in the future, on the 75 going to Croydon.

> *Moves seats again.*

Then there was 'Woman Wearing Leggings When She Shouldn't' talking loudly on her phone about someone called 'Tricky' who kept giving her the runaround.

> *She gestures behind her.*

Then there was 'Smelly Man who Was Cute' and 'Not So Smelly Man Who Wasn't Cute At All' talking about – what else – football.

> *Gestures to the side of her.*

And then there was 'Can't Quite Put a Finger On It Girl' – that could have been me – listening to Trap music – not so much me – but always deep in thought. Always with a furrowed brow, looking out of the window, staring at something, anything, nothing.

Do you see where I'm going with this? I could go on. It's ridiculous, I know. No life. Sad. Living mine vicariously through other people's.

Now New Me – well, I don't go on buses that much. I'm a student. MA. I go on the train. And the tube.

I want to take you on a journey, as part of this tour you're all on. So please indulge me, please live a little vicariously through me while I to tell you all about why I became a student. See me as 'Woman With a Look on Her Face That Could Conquer The World.'

> *Pause.*

Have you noticed my shoulders? They used to do this:

> *Puts shoulders up to ears.*

Now they do this:

Drops shoulders.

Apparently as women we tend to carry the weight of the world on our shoulders. All the stress lies here:

Runs her hands round her shoulder and round to the nape of her neck.

I just realized that it wasn't enough anymore to listen to other people's conversations on the bus. And walk around like this.

Puts shoulders up to ears and walks around. Drops them again.

I wanted to sit in a classroom again and smell the smell of hope and look at other wide-eyed people who believed that all their dreams could come true after a great discussion on how Caryl Churchill became Caryl Churchill. And why debbie tucker green doesn't like capital letters.

I wanted to be in that bubble.

I wanted to talk endlessly about whatever writers talk about in quirky cafes that use blocks of wood as plates, where you can order chai lattes with soya milk.

I wanted to buy a new backpack – half practical but mostly cute to go with my new student look I saw on Pinterest when I typed in "casual looks for university".

I wanted student bars, student unions and student discount.

I wanted that 10 percent off at ASOS.

Walks over to wherever her bag is and gets out a notebook.

I wanted to open my brand new Moleskin notebook and fill it with all the great advice different lecturers gave us on how to rule the world.

Drift off and visualize me sitting in the audience, tucked away at the back –

Points to the back.

And hear my words being spoken out.

Round of applause.

Standing ovations.

I wanted to sit in a room full of other dreamers.

Invisibility is like being a shelf to prop up others. Or like a bookend. Standing firm. And sturdy. You're just there. And yeah, you're needed. You serve a purpose. But it's certainly not the purpose you thought you were meant to be here for.

Faces audience.

"I want to be sturdy." Said no one ever.

"What do you want to be when you grow up?"

"Sturdy, miss."

"Oh baby, I love you. You're so – so – sturdy!" Kisses each other passionately. Here she lies. Wife. Mother. Friend. And sturdy.

Shrugs shoulders up and down a few times, slowly.

Old me. New me. Old me. New me.

To really understand what it was to be the old me, I think you should raise your shoulders up to your ears – please don't *not* do it. Don't be weird about it or shy or self-conscious. I learnt a long time ago that being shy ultimately doesn't serve you well. If I continued to be shy – I wouldn't be here now, would I?

Ok, so shoulders up. Come on. That's old me.

Then drop them.

New Me.

Exhale too. It helps.

Ok – let's do it again. It gets easier, I promise.

Shoulders up.

Shoulders down.

One more time. Together.

Shoulders up.

Shoulders down.

Good. So back to my story.

Pause.

Speaks softly.

Because somewhere amongst all this, I knew it was time to live a different life. A different part of my life I hadn't used yet. That was there, waiting for me to stop listening to other people's conversations and make some of my own.

Voice grows passionately. She grows in confidence. Stands up on a chair. And walks across chairs as she talks.

I wanted my chin to tilt up a little more. Whatever conversation I was in – with anybody – I wanted to be able to nod and say, "yes, yes, I agree" and actually - *actually* know what I was agreeing about. Hold myself in a room. Be witty and well read.

I wanted 'Girl Chewing Gum' and 'Girl With Too Much Hair Gel' one day to know of great inspirational role models who changed history, fought hard, championed others. I wanted their conversations to be about *something* meaningful. *Something* significant.

If one day I have a daughter, I want her to see her mother *own* her intelligence, creativity and passion. She'll know that having this –

Touches her face.

Can be a help or a hindrance – but nothing matters if she doesn't have this–

Puts a hand on her heart.

Gets down from chair and sits down.

I wanted one day for other women like me to sit in a classroom after life giving them a second, third or fourth chance at having another crack at it – and can I dare say it – believe all their dreams could come true after having a great seminar on how I became me?

I wanted to have all the belief in the world that I can be all those Greats that we hear about. And do it my way. Of course I know it's hard out there. But… but being a student again, was one of the best decisions I ever made.

Shrugs shoulders up and down a few times, slowly.

Old me. New me. Old me. New me.

If you have a spare eight and a half grand what would you do with it? Probably not give it all to an institution that gives you no guarantees, no promises. You'll live off 'maybes' and 'possiblys'. You'll flick through old note pads full of conversations on buses you thought were inspiration for a good story.

But a memorable conversation I overheard on the bus once, was that of a man who didn't look like he had that much, ask another man for money. 'Man Who Didn't Have Much' said to 'Man Who Had a Bit More' – "I used to dream of being a pilot, you know?" I decided to get off the bus. I couldn't put a price on my dream.

Moves a chair away from the others. Centre. She sits down with a leg crossed over the other, with her hands on her knees. This is her spotlight.

So New Me - not so sweaty. Still always walking fast. Still constantly listening to other people's conversations. But I did something for me and only me: I jumped.

It's wonderful to learn again. We're always learning, I know that. But for me, I needed to be scared.

And Hopeful.

And excited.

Determined.

And I want you to jump too. I want you to be scared. And hopeful. And excited. And determined.

Shoulders down.

Staying down.

SCENE THREE

LUCY turns to the audience.

LUCY: Okay, so, that was the beginning of our tour.

    And wasn't it brilliant

    Because it reminds me of why I became a student

    Which I'll tell you about later

    But before I do, I hope you are considering your thoughts on whether you think it's important to be a student in the UK or not, ready for our vote at the end of the tour.

    And, on that note, let's go on to our next room to help you continue to decide.

    Walk like me.

> *She does a weird walk, perhaps like a chicken, encouraging the audience to copy her.*

    There's no need to be shy

    You can forget my earlier advice about being serious.

    Follow me.

> *They leave for the next room, LUCY continuing to do the weird walk.*

SCENE FOUR: THE OTHER SIDE BY VEE TAMES

Chairs are set out in rows either side of the room. A central aisle has been created down the middle. A lectern has been placed at the front of the room. A clipboard with handwritten notes is placed on the lectern.

AYESHA, 18, has been invited to speak to prospective pupils as a Student Ambassador for The Student Guide To Being A Student In The UK Tour. She wears her school uniform with a student ambassador t-shirt on top. She waits by the door to welcome parents and students.

Parents and Students file in. AYESHA shakes hands with parents and urges LUCY to help everyone to their seats.

    Is that everyone?

    Great. Thank you, Lucy.

> *She walks up to the lectern and slots herself behind it.*

    Good morning.

    It's an absolute pleasure to welcome you all here as your Student Ambassador for the day.

I'm sorry if I ramble on too much – it's just I've never been put in charge of something before so to be chosen as Student Ambassador for this tour today is a huge honour... so your votes about whether it's important to be a student in the UK or not mean a great deal to me!

You know, I was just thinking about what it was like when I was sitting where you are now. Excited. Nervous. Unsure. It's terrifying... just realizing how fast it's gone – oh god, I'm going off topic....

Oh god, oh god, oh god, I'm so sorry.

> *She looks down at her clipboard, frantically searching for her next point.*

Got it. Right. So, anyway, a little bit about me. My name's Ayesha, I'm 18 and I've just finished my A Levels in Biology, Chemistry, Maths and Further Maths at Chamberlain Sixth Form College and hopefully from September, I'll be studying Midwifery at Birmingham.

Yeah. I can't wait.

When did I join?

Two years ago

Before that?

> *Beat.*

Well...

That's a long story.

Besides, you haven't come for my autobiography

> *Beat.*

I know it's a massive cliché but I'm beyond grateful for what Chamberlain's given to me – I'm serious – I have this sense of achievement, this, this purpose that I've never had before. I came here knowing no one and now I know I can be anyone and anything I want. It's crazy. To think, after everything I've gone throu-

I'm sorry

Did you have a question?

Yes. You. At the back there.

Did you want to ask me something?

> *Pause.*

I see…

Wow, that's…. that's…

God. I... I don't even know how I'm supposed to respond to that.

How could you think that an education is just, just, just some waste of time? This, this rite of passage. A barrier, for god's sake! Nothing has been more liberating for me than being given the chance to study here and start over. Nothing.

>   *Beat.*

When you can't get that education, your life is very much controlled by others – you don't get many choices.

Back home where I come from, it was easy for my brothers to think about the future. It was just outside, ready for the taking. They could just run out and grab it with both hands...

I couldn't. My mother couldn't. My sister couldn't. None of us could. Our future was already decided. Our fates were sealed. With no other future than to produce life and live within the four walls of our home without the chance to have lives of our own.

My friend's uncle was shot for allowing his daughter to go to school.

>   *Pause.*

But I'm lucky I don't have to live like that anymore. Trapped with those four walls.

Now I'm on the other side of those walls, I can be someone with something to say. Something to share. Something to contribute to the world, other than housework and children.

>   *Beat.*

Here, I have my own desk, my own chair. I'm not sharing a classroom with fifty other girls – who aren't even the same age as me.

Here, I don't walk three miles to get to school.

Here, girls aren't sent home every month because they're "unclean".

Here, no one's gonna stop you. Tell you, you don't have the right or you can't do that.

Here, no one's going to shoot me for wanting to learn.

>   *Beat.*

It's not like that where I come from. Back home.

I'm one of the lucky ones. I can be someone important. Someone whose voice can be heard. Someone with choices.

I got lucky.

You did too.

We can't all have the luck of being born in the land of the free.

SCENE FIVE

LUCY turns to the audience.

LUCY: Okay, so, that was brilliant as well.

And I hope you are all thinking that you want to vote at the end of the tour that being a student is important.

Also I just want to remind you that my grade is dependent on that and also I am bound to get a higher mark on my module if you do vote yes

Which brings me to my story....

There is a crash or similar.

Hang on.

What was that?

Follow me.

Quickly.

No loitering.

Please.

This is not a safety drill.

Follow me.

The audience follows LUCY to the next room.

SCENE SIX: NUMBERS BY MIRIAM BATTYE

LUCY: Okay, so, what are you doing here?

You're not part of the tour...

MEG sits. Done. Just about done.

In her hands she has a pen and paper.

She has just suffered a miniature internal eruption.

She throws the paper and pen on the floor.

She looks at the audience. Really eyeballs them.

MEG: This has got to be a wind up.

She breathes in heftily.

This has got to be a –

This.

She scrabbles for the paper, holds it aloft.

THIS.

This is too,

It's too

> *She stops.*

This is taking the piss.

This has taken the piss. Out of me. This. This.

> *She suddenly stands up and holds the paper to members of the audience's faces. It has a complex quadratic equation on it.*

What on earth is that?

Seriously.

No, seriously.

Any ideas?

> *She sits.*

> *She looks at the paper again. She tries to do it. She discards it.*

Look. I know.

I know I'm never getting anywhere if I come at this, jaw clenched, forehead scrunched and head full of Can't.

> *A pause.*

But I Can't.

> *A pause.*

Numbers.

My brain's full of them.

Stuffed.

And heavy with it. Can barely keep my head up

> *She stops.*

I'd like them out, actually.

Yes please.

I'd like to pull them all out.

I'd like to put my hand in my mouth, actually, to the back, actually, reach right in and up into my head and pull everything out.

Yeah.

> *She breathes.*

I know it's just numbers, I know it's just lines on paper but this has got to be a wind up

I mean

I feel like a dog in a pedal bin

I'm sweating blood

I must've at least grown myself a tumour over this

I want them out.

Out, please.

Out of my head.

>*A pause.*

Maths.

Thought I'd left it in Whalley Range with my crap braces and Scott Hunters.

But I'm at school again. I look down at that paper and I'm thirteen. I'm pointless and gutless and about forty percent Vimto. I'm a half-made, partially defrosted being with nothing and everything all at once.

But it's not school any more, is it?

I'm twenty-four, I have to pay for stuff like rent and laundry detergent and bran flakes and I don't measure the success of a weekend on how twatted I can get on two quid, I…

I'm a person now.

I'm solid now.

Stuff matters now.

Oh and no one's rooting for me now either. That's a big one.

>*A moment. She looks at the paper. Suddenly –*

It's not just numbers, actually

Did you know that?

No

It's letters.

>*Her face fills with loathing.*

Algebra.

>*She spits the word out.*

Algebra.

>*A pause.*

They've gone and ruined letters too, now.

>*A pause.*

Those smart people.

The boffins.

Nerds.
They must love it
I think they love it, actually

Those little chaps with their big calculators
Who made all this up
Sods, the lot of them
Boring Sods with no game or
Who couldn't get laid
Couldn't speak, probably
Couldn't string a group of words together
So they found numbers.

Put numbers together in a row and worked out how to twist them a little bit
Made them just a little bit more horrible for everyone
Put a little bit of horror into the world for every man woman and child who's
even been put in a ring with a sum and told to go nuts.

Made problems.
Made up endless problems.

Just so they had something to bloody talk about
To bloody talk to, probably

      A pause.
I want to be a nurse.
Hello, I'm Meg and I would like to be a nurse please.
"Hello, Meg, I think we're going to have to make that really hard for you."
"Meg, we hate you and want you to suffer for this a bit, actually."

      A pause.

      She looks at the paper.
D'you reckon they're laughing at us?
From their little desks up in Boring Sod Heaven
Hell, sorry
Hope it's Hell
Hope it's a Hell made out of School Discos and Blind Dates
Of High School Parties
Hope it's just full of, of, *girls*,
That foreign species

Hope they're struggling
Hope they're just sweating through it
Trying to thread one sentence together
Yeah.
Yeah.

> *A pause.*

> *She leans right in to the audience.*

It's all a lie, you know.
X and Y
It's all bollocks.
A thinly veiled way to gob on the masses
Those masses who thought they were nerds
Our little men with their calculators

They'd laugh, probably
Look what we made these people do
We fooled them
Into thinking this *matters*
Look at them down there
Swearing and sweating their way through simultaneous equations
Look what we made them do.

> *A silence.*

I want to be a nurse.
I don't want to win any prizes.

> *She leans forward, imploring.*

I don't even want to count anything past ten and for that I've got my fingers
I'm good with my fingers
I've got a calculator on my phone for anything more ambitious.
A C.

Just a C, I – .

> *She stops, remembers.*

My mouth got me through Eng. Lit and I was always good at computers
I liked Geography. I liked it.

> *She shrugs.*

But Maths was just. Brutal.

Each day, some new fresh hell.

Some running, jumping, flag waving thump to the ego.

I thought that E was the last I'd see of it.

Never thought it'd be back to rip my heart out.

> *She is overcome. She speaks very quietly.*

I'm not going to get to be a nurse, am I.

> *She takes a stabilizing breath.*

I don't think you understand how actually very bad this is.

No, I said I don't think you understand how actually very not very good this is

This is bullshit, this.

I demand a recount.

I demand a bloody recount

I'm not asking to be...Alan Sugar, right?

I'm not asking for like power or lots of money or even much respect actually

People'll piss on me

I just

I just want to like, wash, and and hold people's hands

Give them, I dunno, injections

Just to like

Be a person a bit, to people

Just help people, I dunno, I dunno, cope?

Cope.

Just, cope.

Can't underestimate the power of a good cope, I

> *She thinks for a moment.*

I'm more than that letter on that paper.

But I'm not, actually.

That is actually all that I am.

> *A moment.*

This has got to be a wind up.

This can't be in the way again.

This can't be in the –

Numbers, it

This can't

This can't actually

This

> *She runs out of steam.*

> *She runs out.*

SCENE SEVEN

LUCY turns to the audience.

LUCY: Okay, so, I'm sorry about that.

That wasn't actually meant to be in the tour

I think she's escaped from an exam

I guess we could justify that by saying....

> *She tries to think of a reason.*

… that's the problem when you don't revise, right?
It's not that the exams are too hard

Or why vocational qualifications are now going to have exams so even if you're not good at exams you still have to do them whatever kind of study you choose

Or that some subjects like Maths are compulsory but others like the arts which get you thinking about life, which maybe is just as important, aren't.

Anyway, I'm not sure I'm going in the right direction my bosses would like me to with this…

But it's okay

Because wait until I tell you about my story

Although, before I do that, I think we should go to the next room

Because I'm sure this room will be better

And then you'll think I'm doing a good job.

And be more open to hearing my story.

I promise.

Follow me.

They leave for the next room.

SCENE EIGHT: REFUND BY MUFARO MAKUBIKA

An office.

The audience enter and assemble behind a desk.

Desk has a PC and phone.

Paperwork stacked high on the desk.

STUDENT enters and sits in front of the desk facing the audience.

STUDENT addresses the audience as if they are sat behind the desk.

STUDENT nervously clutches a bag.

STUDENT: Thank you for seeing me.

Understand you must be busy.

Sent a few emails.

You didn't reply.

That's why I'm here.

Have you read the emails?

> *Pause.*

Thank you for seeing me.

I didn't have an appointment.

Late for work.

> *Pause.*

Seen you before at the Lion.

Always have a staff badge on.

You always order the South African Pinotage.

Don't have to even say, I've learnt.

Didn't know that this was your job.

> *A phone rings.*
>
> *The phone rings again.*

Silence.

The phone rings again.

Are you going to answer that?
Could be a student.
Urgent.

The phone stops.

I'll keep going.
Been waiting a long time.

Pause.

The girl before me.
What's she done?
Don't have to say.
It's a private thing isn't it?

Like when a doctor and patient talk.
Confidential like.
That apply to you?

Beat.

You are not a doctor, I know.
You have authority.
Know stuff about people.

Pause.

Don't like pestering people.
You seem very busy.
I'll make it quick.

Pause.

You've read the emails, right?

Silence.

Take a cheque or a bank transfer.
Either is fine with me.
If it's a cheque.
Make it out to me.

Silence.

If you buy something in a shop and it's faulty you can take it back.

A defective product.

There is a law about that.

A law about returning defective products.

Pause.

Know the law?

Beat.

Great.

That's a statute.

Means it's my right.

You are a business, right?

I know you are a school.

But this is a business, right?

STUDENT's leg starts going.

Look, this degree it's no good.

It's faulty.

Not worth the paper it's written on.

I don't want it anymore.

Paid a lot of money for this product.

Pause.

Sorry about my leg.

Gets going when I'm anxious.

Pause.

I was given your email as the person I needed to talk to.

That's why I got in touch.

Not here to waste your time.

If it's a cheque.

I'll take it now.

I'll go.

Never have to hear from me again.

Pause.

£9000 times three.

I won't claim for the maintenance grant.

Figure I spend that.

Had a beer or two.

I'll let you have that.

Paid my rent.

I won't bother with that.

So that's £27,000.

That'll do me.

> *Beat.*

Why are you laughing?

> *Pause.*

No, no!

This is not a joke.

I'm not laughing.

This is no laughing matter.

Surprised at you.

Being a professional and all.

> *STUDENT takes off his shoes.*

Look at the bottom of these shoes.

> *STUDENT shows the soles of the shoes to the audience.*

There are holes in his shoes.

That's the joke.

Been walking everywhere trying to make this work.

It's no good!

> *STUDENT hits the desk in frustration.*

I have holes in my shoes.

My grandfather had holes in his shoes.

Do you understand?

> *Silence, until it becomes uncomfortable.*

> *STUDENT stands.*

Hang on a minute.

We are not done here.

I've been trying to get this meeting for weeks.

We are not done.

Don't shoo me away, I'm not a dog!

I'm not going anywhere.

Don't you dare shoo me away!

> *Pause.*

May I start again?

I'm trying to remain calm.

> *Pause.*

I've been wanting to talk to you for a long time now.

Maybe we lost each other.

That happens sometimes.

I apologise for my rough manner.

I don't know you.

I've only just met you.

This is really important to me.

> *Pause.*

You've read the emails?

> *Pause.*

Why are you looking at your computer?

> *STUDENT sweeps the computer and phone off the desk.*

> *They crash to the floor.*

Jesus!

What are we doing here?

How are you supposed to help me if you don't know my name?

What kind of a con game are you running here?

You don't even know my name.

People have paid good money to be here.

> *Silence.*

Don't you dare move.
Are you thinking of leaving?
I wouldn't do that if I were you.
I have something in my bag.

> *Pause.*

You don't want to push me.
I don't want to hurt you.
I thought we could talk it out.
Reason it out like adults.

> *Pause.*

Sit down.
Later when you are in the Lion you'll laugh about this.
Drinking your Pinotage, you'll really piss yourself!

> *Pause.*

I'm sorry about this.
I know you report to someone else.
There is protocol to things.
That's why I came to see you.
You understand?

> *Pause.*

I could have you done for false advertising.
Your prospectus promises a lot.

> *Pause.*

These halls are full of people like me.
Dreaming.
Hopeful people.
The very education you are selling us.
Makes us hopelessly envious.
Jealous.

> *Pause.*

I know the maths.
Taught me the maths.

Pause.

You tell me that I need this paper.

Pause.

Stopped dreaming.
Isn't that strange?
I sleep, don't get me wrong.
Sleep for hours on end.
Body feels tired.

Pause.

What do you dream of when you sleep at night?

Pause.

Tell me!

Pause.

Do you dream of holidays in the Algarve?
Children?
Houses?
Or do you just dream of glasses of Pinotage?

Pause.

Last dream I had was serving behind the bar.
That was a long time ago.

Silence.

All I'm asking from you is a refund.
Bought a defective product.
Don't want it anymore.
Want my money back.

Pause.

Maybe I should blow this place up.
Blow it to bits.
You can't go on ripping off people like this.
I won't stand for it anymore.

He leaves.

SCENE NINE

LUCY turns to the audience.

LUCY: Okay, so, that wasn't quite what I was expecting.

I think he may have gone crazy.

Which I think is what happens when you get too much stress

Because did you know that more students are suffering from stress than ever before, for example apparently one University has seen a 50% rise in the number of students seeking counselling in the last year

But that's okay

Because when you hear my story

We'll be back on track

And I'll make sure I get my mark for this tour

Because did you also know women from single parent families statistically have one of the hardest times in education.

But I'm not going to let that stop me.

But before I tell you my story

Follow me

I have to show you one last room

And, to be honest, I'm no longer sure it's going to be fine

But let's go anyway.

Follow me.

> *They leave for the final room.*

SCENE TEN: THE FUTURE OF EDUCATION
BY MONIQUE GERAGHTY

A student stands in the middle of a stage. There is a screen onstage. The student welcomes the audience.

FUTURE STUDENT: Welcome to the future!
Your future

Our future

Problems of paying to study are pounding on a lot of people's minds. Class stars are being replaced with pound signs. These are signs of a kind of change. The educational kind.

But for me studying opens up a myriad of possibilities and opportunities.

Experiencing a different culture and living in a different city is one of the major reasons to continue with education.

> *The student gets out a clicker. We see a projection of wattle waving in a breeze.*

Sat on my tuffet,
Waving golden wattle away.

Melbourne with those tall eucalyptus trees, wafting through four seasons in one day.

> *They click their clicker. We see an image of Melbourne University's gothic-like buildings*

Melbourne University with its castle like buildings and turrets. Feels so much like home from home! Such a scene-setter for building the foundations of your future. Invisible breezes of intelligent thinking, moving to an upbeat tempo around gothic buildings.

> *The student gets out a cd player. They click play. The sound of heavy rainfall is accompanied by a bird's eye view of Melbourne. Note: for the rest of the piece, the student controls the images with the clicker and the sound with the CD player.*

Heavy showers always accompanied by an all-encompassing rainbow. Come thunder clouds or monsoon rains, this city line is matched with rhubarb hues. Scattered colours frame your eye-line and dapple with your perspective, sign posting that you're going down the right path. This myriad of experience, education and adventure! Positively reflecting into puddles as you step into another stride along that yellow brick road.

> *The sound of the yellow brick road.*

All the while I would hop, skip, jump and sprint into action. Complimenting studying with running around the bend of a campus track session.

The student mimics the voice of a sports commentator.

"And she's running around the final bend, will she make it to the next Eucalyptus tree? Twenty seconds on the clock. A soft pink and grey parakeet just zoomed past on her left and to her right, there goes another flock. They're looking determined to make it first to the…"

The sound of Chariots of Fire.

And while I'm sprinting to the finish line in the UK, I'm still envisioning the scenery there. Merging places and spaces that I miss as if my time there exists dually in relation to this hemisphere. Revisiting the vision of business men, briefcase tightly gripped, skipping freely along wide streets. Pretty young girls with painted rainbow streaks, randomly shaven in places as a mark of liberated *individuality*.

During the following paragraph, a series of images of ferocious looking Australian birds fill the screen

Melbourne's landscape is scattered with Alfred Hitchcock's birds. Instead of pigeons, we see large magpies a cackling. Like wicked witches of the west, flying on their broomsticks. Kids a sprinting with their legs a turning. Peddling panicked whilst these beady-eyed birds are circling. Matched with all those purple-pink skylines and off-hand rainstorms. Lightning flashes and momentary thunder clappers. Each accompany the page turn of Frankenstein's mood storm or Nosferatu's winding carriage rides.

Pause in the images.

And it all builds up. All these images and backdrops and sometimes I ponder and wonder. What would "the university experience" have been like if I hadn't ventured further afield. If I hadn't tapped my ruby slippers and just made a dive for it.

The opportunity of immersing oneself in a different education system with a variety of lectures and seminars. Where I could step into the Avant-Garde or Aboriginal Writings or simply tie my trainers that bit tighter. To indulge in a culture in a different hemisphere.

The sound of the yellow brick road again. An image of someone wearing ruby red shoes.

I'd have missed all that and the landscape of friendly faces. The current of encouraging phrases. The culture clashes of this "cosmopolitan metropolis".

Your future road doesn't have to be in Australia's yellow. It can be in the red and yellow of China, the stars and stripes of America!

We see a projection of the Chinese then American flags.

But what's next? Now that studying has changed the way I analyze, theorize, criticize, where do I apply my skillset? University education changes the way you think. Opening up new avenues and future prospects. Grasp opportunity with open arms I say! Turn the key that opens up the box. The way I see this city has changed, altered and elongated.

> *During the following paragraph, we see a sequence of flags from different countries wafting in the wind.*

Studying gives you tools to believe in yourself. To orchestrate what path it is you venture down and curate your own experiences. Practice what you want to be and soon you'll be what it is you've practiced. It isn't all about the purse strings that are attached. It's what you gain from it, where you are going and where you want to be.

> *Pause.*

I wouldn't have gone to Melbourne if it wasn't for studying in the UK and embarking on an exchange and I encourage you to do the same. My hopes for the future? That being a student continues to open up more opportunities and lead to experiencing other cultures. That more people opt to further study. Our future lies in the choices we make in the present. Studying isn't just a good option it's a great option!

> *During the following, we see the original image of wattle wafting in a breeze. Then a series of images as the image expands to encompass an entire landscape, dotted with wattle.*

It is our future!

Your future

The future!

SCENE ELEVEN

LUCY turns to the audience.

LUCY: And, so, that's our tour

And, so, all that's left is to tell you my story

Which is why I signed up to do this tour in the first place, when they told me that they were looking for students who wanted to have their say on what it means to be a student in the UK

Because this is what I wanted to say:

> *She refers to her clipboard.*

When I was nine I came to England from Australia

I know what you're thinking

You can't hear my accent anymore

But it's true

I swear

And in Australia the educational system is very different from how it is here

So I was kept back a year

And everyone kept telling me

You're too far behind

You need to work harder

And when my dad died because he couldn't take moving from Australia to England

And we lost all our money

People just told me

You're too far behind

You can't take the scholarship exam

You're too far behind

And so I worked

And when it came to my exams

I studied in the morning before school

And I studied in the breaks between classes

And I studied at lunchtime

And I studied after school

And I got the best marks in my school

And I went to University

And now I am here

On the brink

Of having a career

And a life in England

And having pulled myself back from the brink

And I am doing what I want

And that is what education gave me

That if I worked hard enough

I could get into the university that I wanted to

And, for a while at least, I could do what I wanted

And I could believe in the possibility of my dreams.

And I hope, I hope that if we really try, we can make that true for everyone

And maybe we can also make the transition from education to work easier for everyone as well

So we can all continue, at every stage of our lives, no matter what our backgrounds are, to work towards the possibility of living our dreams.

This is what the poet Keats had to say:

She gets out a book and opens it.

Had I the heaven's embroidered cloths,
Enwrought with golden and silver light,
The blue and the dim and the dark cloths
Of night and light and the half-light,
I would spread the cloths under your feet:
But I, being poor, have only my dreams;
I have spread my dreams under your feet;
Tread softly because you tread on my dreams.

I think that applies to education as well.

She finishes her story

She closes the clipboard

And, so, that's the tour

And I guess all that's left to say is I hope you enjoyed the tour

And, as you leave, I hope you will vote for whether being a student in the UK is important or not

And if you leave your email address we will email you and tell you the results of the vote

And, if enough people vote, we will send the results to No 10 Downing Street as well

Because maybe that's what being a student is about, believing you can make a difference

And, finally, all that is left to say is to thank you for coming and taking the time to think about this subject matter and to give us a chance, as students and studiers, to share our thoughts

We hope you enjoyed the tour

Thank you

> *The other characters come in.*
>
> *They bow.*
>
> *End of play.*

APPENDIX

EMAIL WHICH CAN BE SENT TO THE AUDIENCE MEMBERS AFTER THE VOTE

Hello,

Thank you for taking part in The Student Guide to Being a Student in the UK.

The vote at the end of our tour revealed that (add result)

It seemed to us that education is an important subject with changes to funding, exams, schools and Universities in recent years and thank you for thinking about this subject matter with us.

Best wishes and we hope you enjoyed the tour!

Lucy
Your Guide
The Student Guide to Being a Student in the UK

CONCLUSION

JENNIFER TUCKETT

We hope you enjoyed and found useful *The Student Guide to Writing: Playwriting*. This project is the second in a series of guides, and later books will provide similar step-by-step lesson plans on writing for film, television, radio and digital media, as well as showcasing the best student work in these forms.

I want to conclude by talking about why we came up with the idea for *The Student Guide to Writing* project.

In 2008, I began teaching at a University in the North of England which didn't teach playwriting. When I arrived, I was told there was no interest. In the first year of the undergraduate playwriting module I set up, eight students signed up. Of those students, two got placements at the Royal Exchange Theatre in Manchester. In the second year of the module, forty students signed up, with two getting places on professional writing attachment programmes and one beating off undergraduate and postgraduate competition to become a finalist for the BBC Future Talent Award. In the third year, eighty students signed up, of which six were produced by the BBC. In the fourth year, we set up the UK's first formally industry partnered MA in Playwriting with three of the region's leading theatres.

I believe it was the access to professional training and insight via the industry partnered nature of the module that changed the culture at that University from playwriting seeming like a world those students couldn't be part of to one which seemed exciting and understandable.

At Central Saint Martins, on the MA Dramatic Writing, we are expanding this work to cover writing for film, television, radio and digital media, as well as playwriting. And, with so many excellent professional training programmes emerging in recent years, it feels increasingly possible for Universities and the industry to work together in training writers and, via doing so, to provide students with the opportunity to learn about who works in the industry and what is being taught on those schemes.

We hope this book publishes for the first time some of the leading industry training in playwriting – for example, Fin Kennedy, Steve Winter, Ola Animashawun, Lucy Kerbel, Caroline Horton and others have never published their teaching methods before.

We hope the winning play by the five winners of *The Student Guide to Writing: Playwriting* competition also provides a script which can be used as an example of the lesson plan and/or be performed, as well as showcasing some of the best student and emerging work in the UK.

The student winners were:

- Schools winner: Vee Tames – a seventeen-year-old student from Colchester, who used the lesson plans to write her first ever play.

- University winners: Monique Geraghty, an undergraduate student from Cheshire who also used the lesson plans to write her first ever play, and Titilola Ige, a postgraduate student from Croydon who secured her first professional productions via the lesson plan work and who was combining studying for an MA with working for the youth charity Reaching Higher.

- Emerging winners: Mufaro Makubika, an emerging writer from Nottingham, and Miriam Battye, an emerging writer from Manchester.

We look forward to providing similar access and showcases for writing for film, television, radio and digital media in future years. Because if writing is about reflecting on who we were, who we are, and who we could be, we hope it's important to help try to ensure that anyone can feel they can be a part of this career and the voices who are being heard.

First published in 2017 by Oberon Books Ltd
521 Caledonian Road, London N7 9RH
Tel: +44 (0) 20 7607 3637 / Fax: +44 (0) 20 7607 3629
e-mail: info@oberonbooks.com
www.oberonbooks.com

A catalogue record for this book is available from the British Library.

PB ISBN: 9781786822154
E ISBN: 9781786822161

Printed, bound and converted
by CPI Group (UK) Ltd, Croydon, CR0 4YY.